STUDYING CHILDREN
Observing and Participating

By Henry E. Draper
and Mary Wanda Draper

Photographs by LeClede A. Arnn

ABOUT THE AUTHORS:

Henry E. Draper is director of child development programs at the Oklahoma State Department of Health and former director of the Institute of Child Development and professor of child development at the University of Oklahoma. In addition, he has held academic positions at several universities and has served as consultant to Head Start and early childhood education programs across the U.S. Dr. Draper earned a Ph.D. from Oregon State University with a graduate fellowship at the Merrill-Palmer Institute and post doctorate study at Harvard University.

Mary Wanda Draper is associate professor of child development in the Psychiatry and Behavioral Sciences Department at the University of Oklahoma College of Medicine. Her teaching career has included preschool and junior and senior high school as well as university teaching and administration. She has served as a consultant for the Oklahoma State Department of Health and for various children's programs including Head Start. Her doctorate was earned at Texas Woman's University with post doctorate study at Harvard University.

Both authors have been instrumental in the development and implementation of several parenting and child development projects. They have worked with young children and parents as well as with students and professionals in the field of child development.

CHAS. A. BENNETT CO., INC.

Peoria, Illinois 61614

Copyright © 1977

**By Henry E. Draper
and Mary Wanda Draper**

77 78 79 80 81 PP 5 4 3 2

ISBN 87002-194-X

Printed in the United States of America

Preface

The study of children means more when one is actually involved with children. First-hand experiences help students and parents see what happens when they apply their knowledge. This book is designed to help the learner develop skills for observing children and participating in their activities. Students are expected to gain greater insight into the development and behavior of children through this approach to studying children.

Three types of learning experiences are presented in this book. These include reading, observing, and participating. The most common type of planned study is usually found to be reading. This is done with a text or a set of references. Reading about children is one good way to study. It is helpful in learning about development, behavior, and child-rearing. Observing children and participating in their activities expands the knowledge and understanding gained through reading. A combination of these three methods offers a more complete learning experience.

Studying children through observing and participating requires preparation. The student must learn what to look for and what to do. Child development principles take on greater meaning when practiced in an actual situation.

Studying children by observation means watching them. It means watching them to discover principles of development. This includes looking at behavior for clues to understanding each child. Observation generally requires the learner to be several feet from the child.

Participation, on the other hand, means active involvement. This includes interacting with one child or a group of children. Participation may include being in charge of children's activities. It may be helping with what is going on. Participation may also mean being with your own children at home.

This book is a package of learning activities. It uses observation and participation experiences in these activities. The experiences allow the learner to work on one or more topics at a time. The activities may be included as part of a course or as independent study. The learning experiences may be used in various ways. Consider the following examples:

As single units. A single unit refers to studying one set of learning activities at a time. Each set is related to a different topic of child development. Here, one may study children by observation and participation limited to this topic. An example is the study of social skills. Single units of study may be used by one or more persons in studying children during a period as short as a few days or weeks. Single units can also extend over a longer period of time. This might include one or more observation and participation experiences each week. The student or teacher, or both, can select those areas of study most appropriate for the learner. Perhaps a series of units will cover a full semester or a year. In this case, more content can be included than in a shorter time period.

A practicum. A practicum experience means the learner participates in children's activities on a regular basis. This may be part of a course or as an independent experience. It might be part of a special workshop or training program. Examples are Head Start and child care services. The practicum may be used by parents at home or in a parenting program.

As a tool for collecting information in a case study. This book can be used to help the learner study one child. This may be done over a short or long period of time, depending on the case. The learner can focus on certain areas of development. The learner can focus on behavior. This will depend on what type of information is needed for the case study.

As an aid in compiling a history or series of daily records. The book helps the learner gather information. This can be done in one or more areas of development and behavior. It may be done on one or more children. This procedure is generally used over a long time period. This book guides the learner in collecting specific information. For example, the learner may be assigned to observe or participate. The task may be to study the behavior pattern of a three-year-old girl. Daily records can be compiled. This may include information gathered while observing the child's behavior. Observations are made until one is able to see a possible pattern. A comprehensive, or very thorough, picture of a child's behavior can be compiled this way. Observations may occur over a long period of time, say for several weeks or months. This serves as a type of history. It helps the learner to actually see a child's behavior taking shape in everyday life.

As a means of studying child development. A study of child development may be limited or very broad, depending on the learner's situation. This book is designed for a person studying child development either alone or in a group.

The study of child development may include only a few or all of the experiences in this book. The learner may use one or more of the above approaches. Again, the book is designed to give the teacher and the learner flexibility. This applies to both the approach and the content.

Video and audio tape recordings can be used with the experiences in this book. This is another way for the learner to study development and behavior. For example, the area of eye-to-hand coordination can be studied by viewing children on video tape. This can be done to prepare the learner for observing and participating. When the learner is involved, clues to this area of development will be more obvious. The video tape can also be used following an observation or a participation experience. It can be used to review and point out certain aspects of children's development and behavior. The video and audio tape method has another advantage. The tape can be stopped at any point. After discussion the tape can be continued. It can also be played as many times as necessary. This makes it possible for the learner to study certain kinds of development and behavior in greater detail. It also makes it possible for one person to see and review his or her own

effectiveness with children. The method provides feedback which can reveal strong and weak points in the learner's behavior. This can be a motivation for improving and changing as needed.

The experiences in this book are planned to help the learner observe and study specific areas of development. Samples of these areas include self-concept, language skills, thinking and reasoning, social skills, and motor coordination. Each experience may be used either for observation or for participation. It may also be used as a combination of both. The experiences have not been pre-numbered. They may be used in the order presented in the book or in any order desired. The material which prepares the learner for each experience has been given a chapter number. The chapter numbers, however, are not designed to influence the order in which the material is used. Chapters 1 through 6 contain general information. It can be applied to all the experiences. Chapter 3 and Chapters 6 through 20 are followed by at least one related experience.

Some of the observation and participation experiences are planned for use in evaluating children's programs. Some areas of program evaluation include goals and objectives, organization and administration, and activities for children.

In addition to students, this book can also be used by persons already involved in working with children's services and programs. These persons may include teachers, directors, assistant teachers, nurses, curriculum coordinators, social workers, and volunteers. Parents can use it to develop better skills in child-rearing. They can learn while interacting with their own children. The learner using this book is expected to become a keen observer. This leads to greater insight into children's development and behavior. The learner is expected to become more effective when interacting with children in both home and community settings.

DEFINITION OF TERMS

The following definitions will be helpful in using this book. Keep in mind that these terms might not be used the same way in other references.

Development. Development is used as a broad term. It refers to any gradual physical or behavioral change in a person. This term can include a combination of such concepts as growth, maturation, learning, and behavior.

Growth. In this book, growth means an increase in size or weight—the multiplication of cells and tissues. Growth causes the body to become larger and weigh more. For example: "The child grew four inches and gained ten pounds last year."

Maturation. Maturation is a change in the quality of a characteristic. A physical increase in size may not even have occurred. For instance, the tissues of the body change in ossification (the changing of cartilage into bone). This means that maturation is occurring. It does not necessarily mean that there has been an increase in size or weight of the bones. Maturation also occurs in mental processes. An example is the ability to distinguish between "more" and "less." When efficiency increases, maturation has occurred. This is true even though no additional knowledge has been acquired. Maturation will be used in this book to refer to a qualitative change. This means a difference that improves the quality. The improvement will apply to physical, intellectual, social, and emotional changes. Maturation will not refer to a quantitative (amount of) change.

Behavior. Behavior refers to any activity. It can be a single act or response. It can also be a series of acts or responses. Good behavior means the child's actions are appropriate in time, place, and circumstance. Misbehavior, on the other hand, means the child's actions are inappropriate. Behavior is a useful term. It helps explain how children act and what they do.

Learning. Learning is any real change in behavior. It is the attainment of knowledge, skills, and behavior patterns. These may be positive or negative. A child who has learned to walk has increased ability to move from place to place. A child who has learned to count can use simple forms of money or divide toys with playmates. A child is also learning when he or she gains attention by being destructive. The child is learning even though decreasing the ability to get along with others.

The following definitions will help clarify the terms used in the observation and participation experiences.

Observation. Observation refers to watching children. It also means noting what they do and say. Observation includes watching adults and others who may be interacting with children.

Participation. Participation refers to being involved with the children in their activities. Participation includes interacting with children as well as observing them at the same time.

Objectives. Objectives are the targets of learning—what the student will gain from the experience. Objectives guide the learner toward a meaningful experience. This experience can bring about change or improvement in the learner's behavior.

Setting. The place, type of situation, persons involved, and time of day make up the setting. This includes basic information. It should be recorded for each experience. The total setting should be described even though the actual observation or participation may include only a part of the setting. For example, a setting might include thirty children although only two children are observed. The setting may be a day care center with five activity rooms although only one is used for observation.

Tasks. Tasks are what the learner will do—the actions of the learner. They may be very similar in content to the objectives. A task is what is to be done in order to achieve the objective.

Evaluation. The evaluation is the process used by the learners to help them see their own progress. Objectives have been identified for the experiences. The learner attempts to achieve these objectives. Evaluating is a way of seeing how much progress has been made. It is a way of deciding to what extent each learner was able to achieve the objectives.

Dedication

To our sisters, Eilene and Catherine

Acknowledgments

Special acknowledgment is given to Lenorah Polk for her contribution to the development of this book.

Appreciation is extended to the staff, children, and parents of the Oklahoma Child and Family Institute, the Native American Center Preschool, and the Children's House in Oklahoma City for their contributions to the photographs. Special assistance was given by George Farrell, Michael Pone, Mary Helen Nelson, Gerald Kidd, and Jane Vaughn.

Table of Contents

Preface 3
Acknowledgments 6
Chapter 1. Introduction 9
Chapter 2. Role of the Observer 15
Chapter 3. Making Observations Meaningful 17
             The Observation Experience 19
             Observing Children 25
Chapter 4. Role of the Participant 33
Chapter 5. Making Participation Meaningful 35
Chapter 6. The Participation Experience 39
             Participating with Children 43
Chapter 7. Selecting Goals for Children 47
             Goals for Children 51
Chapter 8. Learning through Play 57
             Play 61
Chapter 9. Health and Safety 71
             Healthy Children 73
             Promoting Children's Health 77
             Safety 81
Chapter 10. Building a Self-Concept 91
             The Child's Self-Concept 95
Chapter 11. Infancy 99
             Infancy: First Three Months 103
             Infancy: First Six Months 107
             Infancy: Seven to Eighteen Months 111
Chapter 12. Motor Development and Coordination 115
             Motor Development 117
             Motor Coordination 125
Chapter 13. Intellectual Development 133
             Understanding Intellectual Development 137
             Concept Formation 143
             Levels of Representation 153
             Thinking Skills 159
Chapter 14. Language 173
             Language Development 175
             Communication Skills 179
             Language Skills 183
Chapter 15. Social Skills 187
             Socialization 189
             Social Competencies: Daily Living Skills 195
Chapter 16. Emotional Development 201
             Emotions 203
Chapter 17. Guiding Children's Behavior 211
             Guiding Behavior 213
Chapter 18. Creativity in Children 223
             Creativity 225
Chapter 19. Program Administration and Management 229
             Administration: Operating a Children's Center 233

Program Management 239
Program Management: Children's Activities 243
Chapter 20. Evaluating Children's Programs 253
Evaluating Programs 255
Evaluating the Observation and Participation Experiences 261
Selected Bibliography, Annotated 263
Index 265

Chapter 1

Introduction

As you observe and interact with children, you will learn to see them as they really are. You will also learn to see them as they see themselves. One of the most effective ways to learn about children is to see them and participate with them in their most natural setting—the world of play.

Play is as vital and as necessary for the child's development as food, air, and rest. Play is an underlying part of the child's life. You will observe children at play and participate with children during their play activities. During this time you will see the value of play in their development. Children spend more time playing than doing anything else during the early years. Through play the child develops in all areas. Behavior and learning take place as the child plays alone and with others.

Children will give you many clues to their development. They do this with their bodies as well as by what they say. While you work with children, you can develop the ability to be a keen observer.

OBSERVATION

Observation is one of the oldest and most commonly used methods of research. It is basic to the study of children. Observation makes the study of children more meaningful. While observing, you will learn to see clues and to collect information about children's development, including behavior.

Observing and recording what is seen helps you recognize patterns, rates, and stages of development. You will see individual differences. You will also see the effects of environment on each child.

PARTICIPATION

Participating with children and other adults will strengthen your study of children. You will become actively involved in the learning process. Participating is a meaningful way to apply your knowledge. It will help you develop additional child-rearing skills. Participating in activities with children will help you evaluate your own progress.

Observing and participating with children enables knowledge to be put into practice. By watching, you can become familiar with the settings and the methods used in activities with children. Then you can try these yourself.

Conclusions

Conclusions are considered as final judgments about a child's development or behavior. They are usually followed by recommendations. These pertain to specific action or treatment, depending on each case. Conclusions, in this sense, are considered as judgments to be made by professionals. These persons are well trained in such fields as child development, medicine, psychiatry, or psychology. They have qualified experience in these fields. This includes the use of certain techniques for observations that lead to conclusions. This book does not attempt to provide the basis for drawing conclusions or making recommendations.

As you observe and participate with children you will learn to see them as they really are and as they see themselves. Don't you think it would be fun to get to know Alistair?

The book is for use in observing and participating. It is to help increase one's understanding of children. There will be many instances in which the learner will record evidence of a child's development or behavior. There will be many indicators or clues that suggest patterns of behavior, stages of development, and even problems. From these clues, *inferences* may be drawn. Inferences, however, are not the same as conclusions. Notice the difference in the following statements made by an observer.

Inference: The child appeared to be depressed. She did not want to play with other children. She wanted to be alone most of the time.

Conclusion: The child is depressed and withdrawn. She does not have the ability to relate to other children.

Many inferences about development and behavior will be drawn as you use this book. Even though you may collect lots of information about one or more children, you do not have to draw conclusions. You will, no doubt, observe some facts about children's development. For example, we observed that two-year-old Rick stacked three cubes without help. This is a fact. It is not a conclusion about his ability or development. It is an *indication* that his eye-to-hand coordination is developing normally. It also is an *indication* that he enjoys playing with blocks. His attention span *appears* to be increasing. He *seems* to feel good about himself. The following techniques will help you learn about children without drawing conclusions.

Types of Observation Techniques

Observation techniques are useful ways to study children. These techniques serve as tools to help you do a better job of observing. Because of this, they are given a general description in this Introduction. Study of technique should not be the learner's main goal, however. The primary goal of this book is to help individuals increase their understanding of children's development and behavior. The learner, therefore, is cautioned against becoming so concerned with the technique that the study of

children becomes secondary. For this reason, specific techniques as such have not been emphasized in the observation experiences.

You may be interested in developing special skills in certain techniques, however. In this case, you may want to refer to the references at the end of the book for further information. You may want to enroll in a course especially designed for the purpose of developing skills in the use of observation and assessment techniques.

You will notice that some of the experiences apply only to one technique. Others may suggest a combination of techniques. The teacher and the student may even develop additional techniques that are useful for certain purposes of observation. A discussion of four basic types of observation techniques follows.

ANECDOTAL RECORD

The *anecdote* is a written account or *word picture* of one episode in the child's life. It may be combined with a series of other similar accounts. The resulting record provides a more complete picture of a certain child. In this technique the actual situation is recorded step by step. For example: Compare these two reports of the same episode.

1. Karen got angry as she stood up. Her face turned red. She turned to Leo and said in a harsh tone, ''That's my rolling pin! You can't have it.'' She started to grab for the rolling pin! Leo gently handed it to her without a word. Karen went back to rolling out the playdough.

2. Karen suddenly demonstrated aggressive behavior as she encountered Leo in the use of play equipment. She is egocentric in nature.

Which report gives the best description of what happened? Which report does not draw a conclusion on the basis of one episode?

The anecdotal technique requires that you also record basic information about a situation: date, as well as time, of observation; setting; actions of the child and others involved; quotations of what was said; gestures; and tones of voices.

DIARY-TYPE RECORD

A diary-type record may be used for detail descriptions of one child. The descriptions may be written in anecdotal form. They may also be written simply as phrases or sentences. The objective is to describe the child's actions on a daily basis. This technique is very useful to teachers and parents. It is helpful to them in following the progress of the particular child. These recordings describe development over a period of time. The descriptions include how the child is developing and behaving in a series of situations. This technique leads to a greater understanding of a specific child. At the same time, it increases the learner's knowledge of children in general. The basic procedure is to record observations of a child during different periods of the day. These do not all have to be recorded in the course of one day. The observations may include several days. Details are recorded at certain times. These times might include arrival at a children's center, toileting, free play, outdoor activities, music and creative movements, story time, table activities, and dramatic play. Observations are recorded which include the child's actions in small groups, large groups, and individually. Similar observations may combine to reveal patterns of development. A pattern, here, means a predictable way of developing. For example, children learn to sit before they stand, stand before they walk, walk before they run, and run before they skip.

TIME SAMPLES

This technique is similar to the diary-type record except for two points. It is not generally used on a daily basis, and the time for observing is shorter. The time sample is used to study specific kinds of development. It is used in a limited time period and in a given setting. For example, as you work with children you will take note of a certain child for a ten-minute period. The next day, you take note of the same child for ten minutes at another time of the day. You repeat this procedure until you have collected information for five to ten days. By this time you may have gathered information about the child's self-concept, social skills, body control, thinking skills, feelings, and ability to do things. The purpose of this technique is to observe typical development. The child is usually observed for short periods of time during a

variety of activities. When using this approach, one assumes that everything the child does has a purpose, or is a response to something. Physical actions are related to the child's feelings and thoughts. The child's action is important as a part of the total situation. This situation includes persons, things, physical surroundings, expectations, activities, and responses from others. This makes it necessary to note the situation which caused the child to act—not merely the action itself. This technique allows you to collect information from short observation periods. This may take several weeks or months. This information will help you either agree or disagree that a particular child's development or behavior appears to be typical.

The time sampling approach also helps the observer to recognize an individual's pattern of development. Questions to be answered during this type of observation include the following:

- What started the activity—the child or someone else?
- What was the physical setting—room arrangement, outdoor area, equipment, materials?
- What was the social setting—people involved, activities, what was said?
- What were the child's actions or reactions? Did the child succeed with the task at hand?
  What skills were obvious or lacking?
  What did the child say or do to adults; to other children?
  What attention and response did the child receive from adults; from other children?
  What was the child's level of interest? Very interested, somewhat, or hardly interested?
  What was the child's behavior like in group situations?
  What was the child like emotionally? How did the child appear to feel?
  What feelings were expressed? How?
  Did the child show independent or dependent behavior?
- What was the child's behavior following the activity?

CONTROLLED OBSERVATIONS

Controlled observations require systematic recordings of what you see. The recordings may take the form of a description, scale, or a checklist. The observer's attention is directed to *specific actions or responses.* Examples include what the child says or does, facial changes, and hand and body movements.

Description is a valuable recording device. Take this example of observing problem-solving skills. We watched Lisa until she became involved in a problem-solving situation. Here is a description of what we saw. Lisa filled containers with water during water play. Each time she poured water into a container, she opened her mouth wide. When the container was full, she closed her mouth. As she screwed the cap or lid on each container, she followed her hand and finger movements with her eyes. She also made mouth and tongue movements. These motions showed her intense interest in solving the problem of getting the caps or lids on the containers. She used a trial and error method to get the correct top on each container. She would try each top until she found the one that fit. Then she discovered she could open some of the caps by pulling a tab. She then squeezed the bottle and watched the water squirt out. The next observation period, we watched Lisa playing with beans. Many of the same containers were available to her that she had used with the water play. Lisa tried to fill and empty the containers with beans in the same manner that she did with water. She discovered that beans and water could not be played with in the same way. Beans neither poured nor squirted like water did. Again, by trial and error she made a discovery. She had to take the cap off to get the beans out of the container. In both situations we observed Lisa's problem-solving skills. In both experiences Lisa used many mouth and facial gestures which indicate typical development. We saw evidence of the mind and body working together to solve problems.

The purpose of this technique is to collect information about children's *typical development.* This includes sensory and motor abilities, self-concept, thinking, social skills, emotions, and daily living habits. As the observer, you decide beforehand the kinds of behavior to be recorded. Then you must wait until that kind of behavior occurs. Perhaps the kind of behavior for which you are looking will not appear. Perhaps atypical behavior will occur instead. In

either case, make note of it. This technique is very helpful in identifying children with special problems. It is also helpful in identifying those who need help in one or more areas of development.

Scales and *checklists* are additional types of controlled techniques. These methods are generally more objective than anecdotal or diary-type records. Rating scales consist of number scores for certain types of development or behavior present. (An example is item 7 on page 22 of this book in the section entitled ''The Observation Experience.'') This kind of observation is specific. It requires less time in recording than other methods. Details concerning the same type of development can be grouped together. The rating scale technique presents a short summary of information. This is opposed to a long description of details as in other methods. Checklists provide a simple way to record observations. You generally check the appropriate columns according to the instructions. Some checklists contain additional space for writing short comments or for providing a brief statement of evidence about the item checked. (An example is on page 195 of this book in the section entitled ''Social Competencies—Daily Living Skills.'') You are usually instructed to observe a type of action more than once before checking. This helps avoid recording a coincidental activity. Such an activity may not reflect the child's real level of development. For example, an infant may appear to respond to an adult gesture on the first trial. However, unless the infant repeats the response three or four times, it should not be recorded. This could possibly be a coincidence rather than development or a learned behavior.

There is another advantage of a rating scale or checklist. Information can be compared on the basis of the same tool or instrument. For example, you might observe a child three times. When using the same scale or checklist, you can compare the scores for each observation. This also makes it possible to compare a child at various stages of development.

There are limitations to this method. Some traits or areas of development are easier to rate than others. This is because some can be more easily identified. This method requires an accurate instrument (score sheet or rating scale). It is needed in order to record meaningful information about development and behavior. The observer must know exactly what to look for. Each trait or skill must be clearly defined. Otherwise, it cannot be rated or scored accurately. The instrument must be well constructed. Several observers using the same scale in the same situation should get almost the same results.

This method has a further limitation. You must observe the evidence often during the total observation time. Even though you see a particular trait or behavior, you must look even further. You must view the whole situation. Seeing a trait or behavior does not automatically add to one's understanding of the child. It is helpful to be aware of the total situation which brought about the behavior.

Can you see that working with children and observing them leads to a greater understanding of development? Some examples of areas you will see include the following:

• Physical and motor development—growth patterns, eye-to-hand coordination, manipulative skills, and body control.

• Intellectual development—formation of concepts, problem solving, and learning through the senses and active involvement.

• Socialization—getting along with others, feelings about group activities, and adjustment to routines and limitations.

• Self-concept—evaluation of the self within the surroundings, including things and people; how one is treated; what one thinks of one's self; and how one sees the self fitting into the whole situation.

• Emotional development—feelings about one's self and others; attitudes and behaviors which express one's feelings about how things are.

The quality of an observation depends on one's ability to be objective. It depends on accurate recordings of what is actually going on. The quality of participation depends on one's ability to relate to children in a meaningful way. One must have respect for each child's worth and dignity. One must have genuine concern for each child's well-being.

Through play the child develops in all areas.

Play is an underlying part of the child's life.

Chapter 2
Role of the Observer

As you study child development by observing, you will view children in many situations. These experiences will help you learn more about their development and behavior. The following suggestions will help you observe children in a meaningful way.

BE PROFESSIONAL

All observation information must be treated as *confidential*. Observations should neither be left in public view nor shared with others. Reserve observation records for purposes of study. Observations are to be objectively discussed in light of the total situation. Reports of other observers are to be considered with the same purpose in mind.

BEHAVIOR OF THE OBSERVER

As an observer, follow these guidelines:
- NO TALKING PLEASE!!
- Only observe when scheduled.
- Leave unnecessary coats, books, and other personal items outside the observation area.
- Enter the indoor and outdoor areas by the designated places. Be certain to close doors and gates unless requested to leave them open.
- Whenever possible, *sit* to observe.
- Observe from a position which will not interfere with children's play.
- Observe as an individual—groups of observers only draw attention and distract others.
- Dress appropriately for outdoor observation.

Recording Observations

Include the following basic information on each experience:
- Title of the observation
- Your name
- Date of observation
- Time of observation
- Names and ages of children—number of children present
- Number of adults working with children
- Type of situation (public or private nursery,

preschool, kindergarten, family day care home, day care center, private home, other)
- Other information (for example: indoors, outdoors, field trip, cooking, eating, playing, etc.)

In recording observations, follow these general guidelines:
- Read and study about children as much as possible before observing. Make the observation experience more meaningful by preparing yourself in advance.
- Use verbs, adverbs, adjectives, and phrases that describe children's behavior and development. Example: Janie *cautiously crawled* through the tunnel made of chairs covered with a red blanket. Nicole *hesitated* before she *screamed* with a *sharp, shrill* voice.
- Adjust your position in order to hear and see.
- Learn to look at children objectively—*as they are.* Try to see them without ideas that you may have had before working with them or observing them. Avoid thinking about what they *ought* to be doing. This will help you see what they *are* doing. Be aware of your own biases and prejudices. Keep them out of your observations.
- Look for details, such as the following, when observing children at play or at work with others.

  Who approached whom? In what manner? How did the child behave? Describe the following:

  Body position and movement—touch, shove, push, pat, crawl, creep, sprawl, stretch, fling, throw, hit, kick, hug, withdraw, cling.

  Quality and tone of voice—soft, screechy, flat, pleading, strained, whining, moderate.
- When you are only observing, do not get involved with children's activities or the adults in charge.
- Avoid interacting with the children. Do not start a conversation with a child. If a child asks you a question, answer in a pleasant, matter-

of-fact manner. A child may ask what you are doing. Simply say that you are watching children playing.

• Use pencil and paper to jot down notes. Describe what you see in the order that it happens.

• In recording conversation, try to use a child's exact words. Listen to the voice tone as well as the child's language.

• As soon as possible after an observation, read over your notes carefully. Fill in missing information while you still have it in mind.

• Type or write clearly when filling out observation forms.

When you are only observing, do not get involved with children's activities or the adults in charge.

Chapter 3
Making Observations Meaningful

The first observation experiences will provide new learning opportunities. You will become acquainted with the tasks of an observer. Many observations will be needed. They will help you become alert to the child's general surroundings. You will also become alert to the emotional and social climate in which children and adults are interacting.

The settings in which you observe children will vary from one place to another. You will also find different situations in the same place from one time period to another. Your ability to make accurate observations will increase with practice.

The length of an observation period may extend from several minutes to several hours. Authorities do not agree on the ideal length of time for one observation. It depends upon the activity of the child and the ability of the observer.

As a beginning observer, limit the range of what you watch. Watch one child closely for about five minutes. After this, switch to another child. Then change to a third child in the same

Which hand is John using for this task? His eye-to-hand coordination appears to be well developed for pouring his own juice.

Begin by observing one child. On the right you see John, listening to a story. Notice his facial and body features. Note what the child says and does during an activity.

Now what do you see? Observe which hand John is using to hold the needle for threading his necklace. Look at John's mouth. Watch how young children open and shut their mouths as they pursue motor tasks with their hands.

John is enjoying another story. Here, his hands appear to be helping him express thoughts. He appears to be saying something. Do you think John is pleased with the necklace he made earlier? How do you like that cottonball for a touch of creativity?

activity. Notice whether or not the behaviors observed seem typical. It is wise to start with a child engaged in a quiet activity with only a few others involved. For the second observation period, you might choose one activity and watch a group of children for about fifteen minutes. Still, it is wise to make one child the focal point, even when watching a group. Observe the action around that child and the interaction with others in the group. The next time, you might watch a group during a specific activity. Observe the interaction of several children.

A child's behavior changes in different situations. If you are a close friend, the child may act differently than in the presence of someone the child does not know. Therefore, as an observer you must remain objective and passive. You can still project a feeling of warmth into the situation.

Name _____   Date _____

Course _____   Experience # _____

THE OBSERVATION EXPERIENCE

(To accompany Chapter 3)

OBJECTIVES:

- Discuss the meaning and value of observation as a way of studying child development.
- Report specific information about the observation setting.
- Report observation information without drawing conclusions.
- Report your own thoughts and feelings while observing.

SETTING:

Type of situation (care center, family day care home, nursery, preschool, kindergarten, Head Start, private home, other) _____

Other information _____

Number of children present _____   Number of adults _____
Names and ages of children observed:

1. _____   Age _____

2. _____   Age _____

3. _____   Age _____

Time of day _____

TASK:

Observe a children's setting and respond to the following items.

Recording Observations

1. Describe the setting, the place in which you observed. *EXAMPLE: The family day care home was in a large brick home with a fenced backyard. The rooms were large and there was plenty of space for five children to play. The furnishings were clean. The room was bright and well lighted.*

(Continued on next page)

2. List the children's activities that took place while you observed.

3. Report your observations of the following:
a. Safety *EXAMPLE: Dummy plugs were used in electrical outlets; medicine was kept out of sight and reach of the children.*

b. *Supervision or guidance*

c. *Equipment*

d. *Room arrangement*

Name _____ Date _____

(The Observation Experience—continued)

Obtaining Information

4. Observe one child. Answer the following questions:

Child's name _____ Age _____

How was the child dressed?

Did the clothes appear to help or hinder development? Why?

How did the child use his or her body during an activity?

How did the child express feelings? (about one situation)

What did the child do that showed curiosity or interest?

(Continued on next page)

Anecdotal Records (Word Pictures)

5. Observe one child in a specific activity for about three to five minutes. Describe, in detail, what happened.

Evaluating Yourself as an Observer

6. How did you feel while observing?

_____ conspicuous   _____ apprehensive   _____ confident

_____ comfortable   _____ frustrated   _____ adequately prepared

7. Rate the observation experience by circling the number closest to your thinking.

0	1	2	3	4	5

It was confusing.   It was meaningful.

8. What would you do differently the next time you observe in a similar situation?

Name _____ Date _____

(The Observation Experience—continued)

EVALUATION:

1. Explain how observing children helps to gain insight about their development.

2. Why is it necessary to record specific information about children?

3. Why is it important to avoid drawing conclusions about children or their development as a result of one observation?

4. What role do you think your feelings play in observing children?

Name _____   Date _____

Course _____   Experience # _____

OBSERVING CHILDREN

(*To accompany Chapter 3*)

OBJECTIVES:

- Discuss the value of observing children during their early years.
- Describe ways to develop skills in observing children's development.
- Explain how to report accurate observation information.

SETTING:

Type of situation (care center, nursery, preschool, family day care home, Head Start, kindergarten, private home, other) _____

Other information _____

Number of children present _____   Number of adults _____

Names and ages of children observed:

1. _____   Age _____

2. _____   Age _____

3. _____   Age _____

Time of day _____

TASK:

Record your observations of children based on the following experiences.

Observing One Child

1. Observe one child for five to ten minutes. On Chart 3-A record everything the child did. Also record what the child said and what others said to the child.

Chart 3-A
OBSERVATIONS

What the Child Did	What the Child and Others Said

(Continued on next page)

Chart 3-A
OBSERVATIONS Continued

What the Child Did	What the Child and Others Said

Observing any Unusual Behavior

2. Observe the same child for fifteen to twenty minutes. On Chart 3-B list the child's activities. Note any unusual behavior, such as a sudden outburst of temper, crying often, or hitting or kicking others.

Chart 3-B
OBSERVATIONS

List of Child's Activities	Unusual Behavior

26

Name _____   Date _____

(Observing Children—continued)

Observing Adult-Child Interaction

3. Observe adults and children interacting. On Chart 3-C record one situation in detail. Describe the situation and record the words of each person.

Chart 3-C
OBSERVATIONS

Situation	Conversation

Observing Development

4. Observe several children during play. Record information about children's development by completing the checklist on Chart 3-D. Place a check mark (√) beside the kind of involvement you saw. (Notice the examples. They will help you in reporting your observations.)

(Continued on next page)

Chart 3-D
CHECKLIST FOR OBSERVING CHILDREN

Children's Involvement	√	Type of Activity
• Child used thinking skills to solve a problem. *EXAMPLE: Kim wanted a blanket to cover her doll. She went to the kitchen and found a towel to use for the blanket.*	√	*Playing with doll*
• Child opened mouth when trying to open a container or take objects apart. *EXAMPLE: Randy opened and shut his mouth when trying to open and shut scissor blades.*	√	*Cutting with scissors*
• Child used whole body in activity.		
• Child's tongue and lips moved while painting.		
• Child appeared to feel good about self.		
• Child followed the example of another child or adult.		

(Continued on next page)

Name _____ Date _____

(Observing Children—continued)

Chart 3-D
CHECKLIST FOR OBSERVING CHILDREN Continued

Children's Involvement		Type of Activity
• Child looked at adult for approval.		
• Child looked at adult for recognition or praise.		
• Child corrected another child.		
• Child repeated what an adult said.		
• Child asked questions about something of interest.		
• Child explored through the senses—seeing, hearing, touching, feeling, tasting.		

(Continued on next page)

Chart 3-D
CHECKLIST FOR OBSERVING CHILDREN Continued

Children's Involvement		Type of Activity
• Child purposely acted to get attention.		
• Child expressed feelings with face and body gestures but not with words.		
• Child expressed feelings with both gestures and words.		
• Child used own body to solve a problem.		
• Child showed the correct use of concepts or ideas through play (such as shapes, color, size, numbers).		

EVALUATION:

1. Why is it important to observe children during the early years?

Name _____   Date _____

(Observing Children—continued)

2. Give five examples of children's development that can be observed.
   a.

   b.

   c.

   d.

   e.

3. Explain why it is important to observe the same child over a period of time.

4. What is the value of observing several children in the same setting?

5. Discuss the qualities of an accurate observation.

Chapter 4
Role of the Participant

Studying children becomes very exciting when you participate in their daily activities. You will actually have a part in each child's development. As you participate with children you will notice their levels, abilities, and their limitations. You will see and understand that each child is a unique person. Each has dignity and worth regardless of age, race, and family or cultural background. The following suggestions will help you get ready to participate in child development experiences.

Prepare yourself for participating by reading and studying about children. Look for clues to children's development and behavior as you observe them.

BE PROFESSIONAL

You are responsible for knowing what to do as a participant. Visit with the person in charge of the children before you participate. Whether in a private home or in a children's center, you have certain tasks that will be expected of you. Talk about policies beforehand. For example, you need to know about such items as coffee breaks, type of clothing to wear, transporting children in private vehicles, telephone communications, receiving parents or visitors, being absent, and reporting accidents.

BEHAVIOR OF THE PARTICIPANT

As a participant, follow these guidelines:
- Participate at the time you are scheduled.
- Arrive on time and leave after your tasks for the day are completed.
- Get on the child's level. This may require that you sit on the floor, kneel, or sit in a child-size chair.
- Allow children to do things for themselves.
- Set a good example for children to follow. Express yourself honestly and in a simple manner.
- As you interact with children, be yourself.

- Ask children simple questions to learn how they think and reason.
- Give children honest and simple answers when they ask questions.
- Talk with children in a clear and easy-to-understand manner. *Avoid baby talk!*
- When helping children direct or redirect their behavior, be kind but firm. *Never* use *harsh physical* force with a child.
- Ask for help when you need to in order to carry out your role. Follow the program plan provided by the center, or instructions provided by parents in a home setting.
- Dress for comfort, wearing clothes that are acceptable to the center or home policies.

RECORDING YOUR EXPERIENCES

Include the following identification information for each participation experience:
- Type or write clearly.
- Use the child's exact words when recording conversation.
- Keep a note pad handy. When you are not directly involved with the children, jot down notes that will help you remember details later.
- Describe what you see in the order that it happens.
- As soon as possible after the experience, read over your notes. Also fill in missing information while you still have it in mind.
- Look for clues to children's development. For example:
    How does a child use both body and thinking skills to solve a problem?
    Does the child or adult initiate the activity? How does the child respond to requests from adults and from other children?
    What does the child do and say when wanting information about some activity?
    What is the child's self-concept like? What clues can you see and record that reflect how the child thinks and feels?

Chapter 5
Making Participation Meaningful

As you participate in children's programs, you will be able to study development. You will study such general areas as physical and motor, intellectual, social, emotional, and self-concept. There will be many questions to answer as you learn about each child.

Make note of the child's *general appearance.* How is the child dressed? Do the clothes appear to help or hinder development? Are the child and clothing clean? Does the child appear to be healthy? Is the child alert? Note height in relation to weight and age. Notice the child's body movements. Are they quick or deliberate? How is coordination in crawling, walking, running, jumping, and throwing? How does the child express feeling with words and with the body? Does the chid tire easily?

Clues to *intellectual capacities* (thinking skills) can be found in the child's ability to follow directions. You will find clues in the way ideas are expressed or used. What are the things which interest the child? Does the child appear to be curious? Does the child explore by using the senses and the body? Is the child aware of details? Give specific examples. How well does the child remember? What are the clues? What problem-solving ability do you see?

What are the child's *relationships* with other children? What are clues to the child's concept of self? How and when does one child relate to another? How does the child contribute to group activity? In what way does a child avoid others? In what way do others avoid this child? Give examples of how the child gets along with adults. Is the child in constant need of adult help? Give examples.

In the area of *emotional development,* notice the child's feelings. How does the child express these feelings? How is joy or anger expressed? Is the child frustrated? Does the child use the whole body in expressing some feelings? How does the child react to others' frustration? Give

Lesa enjoys having Jacquelyn nearby, even though she insists on putting the puzzle together herself. Notice how Jacquelyn gets on the same level with Lesa. Can you see how this makes eye contact and communication easier?

John enjoys the challenge of exploring a stacking tower of colorful squares as his friend encourages and reinforces his efforts. Even though this is her first participation experience in this setting, Jacquelyn is relaxed. John also feels comfortable with her.

Stormy is on hand to help children, but she allows them to do as much as they can for themselves.

Notice how Taryn communicates thoughts and feelings through facial expressions and body gestures. Do you think this is a time to get involved with Taryn, or a time to let her experience very personal feelings?

examples of the child's need for personal approval. What amuses the child? Do you see emotional tension, such as constant nail-biting or outbursts of feelings? Does the child seem to hold feelings inside? Does the child's body seem to be tense? Give examples.

Your first participation experience will bring you into contact with both children and adults. You will have many opportunities to use your knowledge and understanding about children.

You may feel somewhat uncomfortable the first few times you are involved with children. Gradually, however, you will begin to enjoy these experiences. Make use of all your talents. These will be helpful in participating with children. For example, if you play a guitar or other musical instrument, you can have fun singing and doing music-related activities. And if you can't play an instrument, you can always play the record player or tape recorder! Children can use your help—from the carpentry and woodworking area to planting a garden or cooking a meal.

Be prepared when you enter a participation experience. Talk with someone in charge. Find out what is expected of you. Learn as much as you can about the center or home. Do this by talking to staff or parents who are responsible. Learn what is planned for children's activities. Find the answers to the following questions:

• What time will you be expected to arrive and depart?

• What will you be doing while you are there?

• To whom are you responsible?

• How many children will be involved?

• Do you know the children's names?

• Can you get a list of the children's names and ages?

• What are the goals of the program? Of the home?

• Do you have the address and phone number of the center or home where you are participating?

You will have many opportunities to use your knowledge and understanding about children.

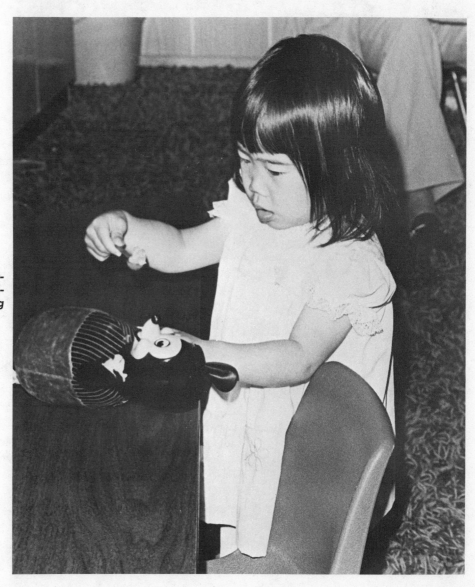

In the area of emotional development, notice the child's feelings. How is joy or anger expressed?

Chapter 6
The Participation Experience

Your knowledge and skills in child care and development will increase as you work with children. This is true whether you are a parent, a baby-sitter, or a participant in a children's program. You can learn more about children by interacting with them. Your appreciation for children will also increase. You will see how they develop and why they behave the way they do. One of the greatest rewards for understanding children is your enjoyment of being with them.

As a participant, your first responsibility is to the children. Their safety, health, and development are the main concerns. All activities and experiences involving children should be aimed at these concerns. Young children think according to their own logic. You must be willing and able to see each situation from the child's point of view. Each child must be treated with dignity and respect, even when things go wrong.

The following thoughts about how children learn and develop will help you in your tasks of caring for and interacting with children:

- All children develop in a logical step-by-step process. (For example, the child learns to sit, then walk, then run, then skip.)
- Every child develops at an individual rate and in a unique way. Some children develop much sooner, some much slower, than others.
- Children usually learn best in a natural and relaxed setting without pressure from adults.
- Children are curious and have a natural desire to explore. They want to discover the world around them. (This is why they often get into things that upset adults.)
- Children learn through their senses of touch, taste, smell, sight, and sound.
- They learn with their bodies as well as their minds. (They like to crawl into things. Watch them open their mouths as they try to open lids on jars and other objects.)
- Children learn best by being active.
- Children have their own logic. They do not think like adults. They see things from their own point of view. They believe what they see. They cannot think from someone else's point of view before about age five to seven years.
- Children enjoy the warmth and care they receive from adults and older children. They learn to love by being loved.
- Children respond best to those who are relaxed and comfortable around them. (Children can sense when adults are frustrated or upset.)
- Children need help in setting limits. This is especially important for very young children. They need limits to protect their health and safety. They need help to feel secure, while they learn to explore.
- Children do not always use good judgment. They are still in the early stages of learning.
- Mistakes are a natural part of the child's learning process.
- It is better for children to ask lots of good questions than to be taught all the right answers.
- Parents are the greatest influence on their children. Children learn more from their parents than anyone else.

When you participate in children's activities keep the following suggestions in mind:

1. *Be a facilitator*—one who makes it possible for children to learn and develop. Respond to children according to their needs and requests. They often give clues about what their interests are.

2. *Prepare the environment* (rooms or play areas). Children need freedom to choose experiences that promote their development. They need a safe and healthy place to play and live.

3. *Encourage children* to explore and discover. When you see they are interested and curious, help them feel free to go ahead.

4. *Let children know you have confidence in them.* They need to experience the feeling that someone thinks they can succeed. They need support to try again.

5. *Get on the same level* as the children. You may have to kneel or sit on the floor.

6. *Use simple language* as you talk with chil-

While participating, look for ways children show their thoughts and feelings. Can't you imagine Robin saying, "I can do it myself"? Observe Don Paul's facial expression and hand movements. Don't they seem to indicate his eagerness to help Robin succeed? Participation will be more meaningful for you and the children as you become aware of children's needs and abilities.

Children depend on you to answer their questions. They also need your recognition and approval as well as your encouragement.

You can provide opportunities for children to expand their knowledge and ideas through play as you talk with them. Give children time to initiate activities and exploration on their own.

dren. Speak clearly and slowly enough for each child to hear and understand you. Avoid slang and baby talk.

7. *Allow children to be themselves.* They need freedom to express their thoughts and feelings. This can take place through such activities as art, dramatic play, creative movements, and sand and water play.

When you participate with children in a center or a private home, be sure you and the adult in charge have a common understanding about your role. Find out what is expected of you and what you can expect. Become familiar with the plans for the day's activities.

• Be on time.

• Wear clothes that are comfortable and suitable for active play with children.

• Be prepared. If you are in charge of certain activities or materials, have everything ready ahead of time.

• Put your heart, as well as your mind, into your involvement with children.

• Evaluate your experience. Ask yourself how well you accomplished the expected tasks. Was it a meaningful experience? What went wrong? Why? What would you do differently next time? What was the most successful part of your day? Why?

Jane helps children enjoy a variety of experiences. Here they see the magic of popcorn in the making.

Let children know you have confidence in them. They need to experience the feeling that someone thinks they can succeed.

Encourage children to explore and discover. When you see they are interested and curious, help them feel free to go ahead.

Name _____ Date _____

Course _____ Experience # _____

PARTICIPATING WITH CHILDREN

(To accompany Chapter 6)

OBJECTIVES:

- Discuss the value of participating with children in their daily activities.
- Describe ways children develop through play.
- Identify ways to study children through participating in their daily activities.
- Report your own thoughts and feelings while participating.

SETTING:

Type of situation (care center, family day care home, nursery, preschool, kindergarten, Head

Start, private home, other) _____

Other information _____

Number of children present _____ Number of adults _____

Names and ages of children observed:

1. _____ Age _____

2. _____ Age _____

3. _____ Age _____

Time of day _____

TASK:

Participate in a children's program and report the results of your experience.

Preparation

1. Report the following information about your participation experience.

    Number of children in the situation where you participated _____

    Number of adults in setting where you participated _____
    Program planning:

    Had you met with the staff previously?   _____

    Did you know what activities were planned?   _____

    Did you know what was expected of you?   _____

    Did you prepare for the participation?   _____

    How long (in hours) was the experience?   _____

    2. Did you prepare materials or activities to be used with the children? Yes _____ No _____
What did you do?

(Continued on next page)

Participating

3. How did you get acquainted with the other adults?

4. How did you get acquainted with the children?

Learning through Participating

5. List three things you learned about children from this participation experience.
   a.
   b.
   c.
6. Identify four areas of development that children experienced through play.
   a.
   b.
   c.
   d.

Evaluating the Experience

7. What was the most enjoyable part of the participation experience?

8. What was the most difficult part of the participation experience?

(Participating with Children—continued)

9. How did you feel while participating? (Check the appropriate terms.)

_____ conspicuous   _____ excited

_____ out of place   _____ adequately prepared

_____ afraid of making a mistake   _____ inadequately prepared

_____ apprehensive (unsure)   _____ in the way

_____ frustrated   _____ important

_____ confident   _____ naive

_____ comfortable

10. Rate the participation experience.

```
      0       1       2       3       4       5
```
It was confusing.   It was meaningful.

11. What would you do differently the next time you participate in a similar situation?

EVALUATION:

1. Explain the necessity for participating with children in order to gain knowledge and insight about their development.

(Continued on next page)

2. Give four examples that explain the value of play in the life of a child.

   a.

   b.

   c.

   d.

3. Give three examples of how participating in a children's program helps in the study of children's development.

   a.

   b.

   c.

Chapter 7
Selecting Goals for Children

Goals are the overall targets we are aiming to accomplish. When planning a children's program, one must decide what goals are most appropriate for children. Parents must be concerned about the goals for their children both at home and in community life. Individuals who work with and study children must be aware of goals for the children. In some cases, goals are easy to identify. They may be posted on a center's wall. In other cases, goals are implied. One must then observe the activities and the program to see what goals are actually promoted.

Two challenging questions face those who care about children:

''What kind of people do we want children to become?''

''How can children be assisted to reach their potential without detracting from each one's uniqueness?''

The family, the school, and the community are important. Often they provide opportunities which promote the development of each child's potential. Unfortunately, situations also exist which detract from the child's ability to achieve optimal development.

Generally, we agree that we want all children to be active, happy, and productive. We want each to become an autonomous individual. We want each to live a meaningful life with others. We want children to feel good about themselves. We want them to recognize their unique qualities, worth, and dignity as persons. Children need to be:

- Healthy and safe
- Well coordinated
- Able to relate and communicate with others
- Able to function intellectually—think clearly
- Positive in thoughts and feelings about themselves

There are many processes that lead to the child's total development. For example, creative expression, learning through the senses, independence, thinking skills, and social skills are all areas of concern. It is a challenge to decide which areas should receive the highest priority—which are the most important.

Deciding on a *set of goals* requires study and discussion. One way to begin is to list the characteristics you think are most important for the children involved. Share ideas and consider suggestions from others. Keep in mind that everything which is appropriate for the child may not receive equal consideration. When planning a children's program, four to eight major goals are usually identified. They are selected for having the most importance. Other goals may be accomplished but are not the main targets. The selected goals, however, provide the basis for planning children's everyday involvement.

Children develop by active involvement and communication with others. Because of this, meaningful experiences are especially important to them. Within a framework of goals, ex-

Each child needs to develop a positive self-concept.

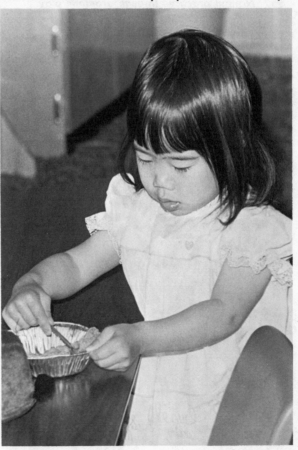

Language and social skills are meaningful in every child's life. Lisa and Amy learn such skills as they play.

Daily living skills take on meaning at an early age. Nathan practices through dramatic play.

periences become meaningful. For this reason, situations and activities for children should be planned to meet these goals. In a well planned program, children can become productive, effective, and happy individuals.

Once a goal has been established, it is important to follow it. It may be necessary to try more than one method of reaching that goal. Take an example of nutrition as a goal for children. Let's see how adults can help or hinder the child's developmental process by changing goals. Almost everyone agrees that it is important for a child to receive the nutritional benefits of vitamins and minerals which come from spinach. But, what happens if a child does not like spinach? Is it possible to substitute other foods which contain the desired nutrients? Parents often require the child to be obedient. This shifts the goal from nutrition to discipline. Can you see how easy it is to lose sight of the major goal?

In this case, the parent turned from nutrition to discipline, from the main goal to a secondary one. As you gain experience with children you will be able to place goals in their order of importance. Avoid many unnecessary struggles and conflicts with children by knowing what you are trying to achieve. When one approach to reaching a goal does not work, try other methods. There are more alternatives for reaching that goal.

Let's return to the example of nutrition. Notice how the child's progress can be hindered if goals are changed. Remember, the major goal is meeting nutritional requirements. While the child is eating or being fed, affection and concern can be shown by the adult. This helps the child develop security and a positive self-concept. However, this feeling may be lost if the adult is determined to have the child eat the spinach. The adult may insist the spinach be eaten because it is good for the child's health, whether the child likes it or not. Can you see how this may hinder the child's development? In addition, the child may lose confidence in the adult if the goal continues to shift to parental control.

The child may be persuaded to eat the spinach. Even though nutritional benefits are gained at this particular meal, progress may be hindered in reaching goals at another time. Behavior patterns may also develop at mealtime which can hinder progress. These patterns may eventually prevent meeting nutritional goals with ease. It may take a great amount of time and effort to help the child regain dignity, self-respect, and confidence after a "showdown" at the table. This kind of situation also detracts from the adult's ability to influence the child's reasoning and thinking process. To help prevent such a situation, a time should be planned to help children develop self-discipline, if needed. It should involve situations and activities appropriate for that purpose.

Activities help children develop in all areas. The use of toys, games, clothing, and chil-

Motor skills combine with thoughts to create interesting objects that have meaning for children. Can you see how an organized environment also helps to accomplish goals for children's development?

dren's furniture helps in this process. Daily activities such as playing, eating, listening, and working all contribute in one way or another toward certain goals. The child's relationship with others influences success or failure in reaching goals.

49

GOALS FOR CHILDREN

(To accompany Chapter 7)

OBJECTIVES:

- Define *goals* for children.
- Describe ways in which a children's program promotes goals for children.

SETTING:

Type of situation (care center, family day care home, nursery, preschool, Head Start, kindergarten, private home, other) _____

Other information _____

Number of children present _____   Number of adults _____
Names and ages of children observed:

1. _____   Age _____

2. _____   Age _____

3. _____   Age _____

Time of day _____

TASK:

As you observe or participate in a children's program, respond to the following items.

Goals

1. Identify and list the goals for the children in the setting in which you participate or observe. (Goals may be discovered in any of the following ways. You may see a list of goals posted. The goals may be obvious by the room arrangement and equipment provided. The staff may tell you what the goals are. The goals may be subtle and reflected by the nature of the program.)

GOALS

(Continued on next page)

Room Arrangement

2. Does the room arrangement appear to support the goals for the children? Explain. Draw a sketch of the room arrangement.

Interest Centers

3. List the interest areas or activity centers for children.

(Goals for Children—continued)

Activity Plan

4. Give a general outline of what the activity plan includes for the children. Is the focus toward achieving the goals for the children? Explain. (For example, some programs focus on teaching music rather than on the development of language skills through music.)

Focus of Program

5. Were the goals child-centered, staff-centered, or activity centered? Give your comments about each of the following with respect to this question.

   a. Special interest themes were used by adults in children's activities (topics of interest such as plants, animals, transportation, food). Yes _____   No _____
   Comments:

(Continued on next page)

b. Children had opportunities to explore their interests and develop their abilities through the use of equipment, materials, and interest areas. Yes _____ No _____
Comments:

c. Adults attempted to control the children's behavior. Yes _____ No _____
Comments:

d. The program was planned to meet many different needs of children with adults responding to each child throughout the day. Yes _____ No _____
Comments:

e. The room arrangement and materials were planned in advance. Adults allowed children to choose activities from many possibilities. Adults worked with children in all areas. Yes _____ No _____
Comments:

(Goals for Children—continued)

EVALUATION:

1. Assume that you are directing this children's program next year. What broad general goals would you want the children to achieve? List at least four and no more than six.

    a.

    b.

    c.

    d.

    e.

    f.

2. What kinds of activities (curriculum) would you plan in order to achieve these goals?

Chapter 8
Learning Through Play

The early years of childhood are filled with the excitement of learning through play. Basic learning skills emerge as early as infancy. With challenging and stimulating play, many developmental skills are likely to be mastered. Play is a medium for mental, physical, emotional, and social development. Children increase their basic sensory and motor abilities through play. Without adequate play experiences, a child may have difficulty with later tasks that require abstract thinking.

Sensory activities involving touching, tasting, seeing, hearing, and smelling help children build foundations for thinking and learning. Adults can provide opportunities for such activities. These encourage children to use their senses in exploring their world.

Early in life the baby begins exploring with the mouth. The baby's mouth is not only for sucking and eating, but for releasing tension and for pleasure. Sucking a thumb, or a toy, may show that the infant feels pleasure. It may also show that the child is learning about the surroundings through touch, texture, and taste. Through finger-sucking, the infant discovers there are feelings in both hands and mouth. Can you see how the baby learns to use more than one sense at the same time?

By about three months, infants can hold their hands in front of them and study them as playthings. Of course, these hands quickly go into the mouth. Coordination skills begin as the infant uses hands and eyes together in various play activities. Reaching for and grasping a toy is usually mastered by about five months. This is followed by banging an object on a hard surface to achieve a noise. The senses of touch, sight, and hearing come into action and help the child learn through play.

Hearing, like vision, is quite well developed at birth. Both of these senses are used in play. At this time the child has daily opportunities for viewing objects and for reacting to sounds. When a child turns toward a sound, a coordinated skill is being developed. The child directs the body movements, the listening concentra-

tion, and the eye focus toward the source of the sound. When children learn they are actually making a sound, their own voices become a part of play. They learn that sounds can be repeated time and time again.

Eyes are used for exploring as well as for enjoying toys and play. Even young infants show interest in patterns and soon follow objects with their eyes. Colorful objects or sunny shadows on a wall help the baby learn and develop through the senses.

Children develop thinking skills as they play with toys and with other persons. They explore the world about them by using their bodies and their senses. During early infancy, children do not know the difference between themselves

Like Ramoan, boys and girls both enjoy a variety of play activities. They need many experiences in which they can freely express and act out feelings and thoughts.

Children develop friendships and social skills as they play. They also experience opportunities for thinking and motor skills.

and others. However, with play experiences and contact with others, they gradually begin to see themselves as separate persons. Children first learn to communicate through their senses and body movements. Later they use language.

Early play begins with the child's own curiosity. However, play is most beneficial when it includes others. Family members and friends help children develop their first social skills.

Play helps children develop basic ideas. These are needed for logical thinking and for understanding about the world around them. For example, children learn to *classify* objects by putting things together that are alike. They soon separate things that are different. Playing with a variety of grocery containers is an example of the way children develop concepts of classification. Watch them group the tomato cans in one place, the milk cartons in another place, and the cereal boxes in a third group. They soon subdivide these items when they notice the labels are different. They do this even though they cannot read. Dishes used in playing "house" are often separated into classes by color or by shape. Before about three or four years of age, most children handle only one concept at a time. So, do not expect them to separate objects by shape, color, and size at the same time. They usually start with shape. They begin to place objects such as cups to-

gether, nails together, buttons, and so on. Later they grasp the idea of color even before they can name the colors. Gradually they notice differences in size.

As children recognize the gradual increase in sizes of objects, they put them in order according to size. This orderly arrangement is called *seriation.* An example of this experience is playing with empty cans of varying sizes. Very young children will manipulate the cans by trial and error until they succeed in getting one to fit inside another. More experienced children can *mentally manipulate* the cans without handling each one. They can make the correct choices for placing the smallest can inside the larger one and so on until all the cans are nested. This mental manipulation depends on both the maturation of the children and their experiences during everyday life.

The idea of how objects fit into space, or *spatial relationships,* emerges with play. Children are especially interested in their own bodies. Play helps them learn how their bodies fit into space and relate to other objects. An example of the desire for such an experience is the girl who ran to her toy box, dumped all the toys on the floor, and climbed into the box. She knew what to do with the box as far as she was concerned. All the toys crammed into the box held no interest for her. On the other hand, the

George facilitates Jill in further exploration through play with art materials.

Can you see how children learn and develop through play when adults __prepare__ the environment, __facilitate__ activities, and __encourage__ children to explore?

empty box itself served as an exciting and meaningful object for play.

The concept of time is difficult for children to grasp. The three or four year olds may learn to memorize the numbers on the face of a clock and the system that shows the "time of day." Still, they probably do not understand the idea of passing time. However, they can grasp some time concepts. Eating and sleeping are two times that children are concerned about. They often learn to judge the passage of time in such areas as these. Routines for daily activities also help children develop ideas about time. Most young children can tell you, without a clock, when it is time for certain television programs that have meaning for them. Young children do not have a clear understanding about time as it relates events such as birth. They may know which brother or sister is older but are confused as to who was born first. They also have difficulty judging time as it relates to distance in travel. For example, three-year-old Karen asked her father, as they left Chicago to drive to

Cleveland, how long the trip would take. Five minutes later she asked, "Are we almost there?" Children have their own logic. It is usually based on what has meaning for them. Another example explains this. Four-year-old Jim was traveling from Texas to California with his family. He asked his mother how far it was to California. She responded by saying about 1400 miles. He said, "No, I mean how many *sleeps* until we get there." Play gives children ways to experience the passage of time in activities that have meaning for them.

Children's play means more to them when they use real objects and have firsthand, concrete experiences. A real doll means more to a child than a picture of a doll. Playing "house" means more than listening to a story about mother or father and brothers and sisters. Manipulating a set of nesting cups means more than watching a television show explaining the idea of seriation to young children. Hammering pegs into slots or glueing pieces of wood scraps together provides real experiences in learning spatial concepts. Pouring sand through a funnel is a problem-solving experience. It is interesting, for instance, to see what happens if a thumb is placed over the narrow funnel outlet.

Concrete play activities using real objects are aids to development. Following this, children gradually begin to use symbols and more abstract ways of dealing with their world. Pictures, sounds from unseen objects, numbers, letters, and stories begin to take on meaning. This is true only after children develop basic skills for thinking through meaningful play with real objects.

Meaningful play with real objects aids children in developing basic thinking skills.

Name _____ Date _____

Course _____ Experience # _____

PLAY

(*To accompany Chapter 8*)

OBJECTIVES:

- Discuss the value of play in the child's development.
- Describe ways children learn through play.
- Identify five examples of play that contribute to the child's development in areas of large muscle control, thinking skills, use of the senses, language skills, social skills, and eye-to-hand coordination.

SETTING:

Type of situation (care center, family day care home, nursery, preschool, Head Start, kindergarten, private home, other) _____

Other information _____

Number of children present _____ Number of adults _____

Names and ages of children observed:

1. _____ Age _____

2. _____ Age _____

3. _____ Age _____

TASK:

As you interact with children or watch them, evaluate their play experiences.

Dramatic Play

1. List three examples of how children pretended or played the role of someone in a dramatic play situation. (These examples can often be observed as children play in the home-living area or large block area.)

    a.

    b.

    c.

(Continued on next page)

2. In one of the above situations, describe what a child acted out. What did the child say and do?

Concepts and Ideas

3. On Chart 8-A list five play experiences that helped a child develop concepts or ideas about objects or situations.

Chart 8-A
DEVELOPING CONCEPTS AND IDEAS

Play Experience	Concept or Idea
a.	
b.	
c.	
d.	
e.	

Name _____ Date _____

(Play—continued)

Problem Solving

4. Describe a specific situation in which a child solved a problem through play. *EXAMPLE: Jill was making cookies with playdough and wanted to cut them into shapes. There were no cookie cutters available because the other children were using them. Jill found a small can in the store area. She used it to cut out her cookies. Then she went to the housekeeping center and found a fork which she used to press each cookie to form her own design.*

5. Describe a situation in which more than one child created a problem. What happened? Were the children allowed to try and solve their problem? What did the children do? What did the adult do? What would you have done if you were in charge?

(Continued on next page)

Eye-to-Hand Coordination

6. List four play activities that helped children develop eye-to-hand coordination.

a.

b.

c.

d.

Listening Skills

7. Explain how children had opportunities to develop their listening skills during such activities as story time, music time, use of record and tape players, and finger plays.

(Play—continued)

Social Skills

8. Give two examples of how children had opportunities to develop skills for getting along with each other through play.

   a.

   b.

Language Skills

9. Describe what happened during play that directly contributed to a child's development in the area of language skills.

(Continued on next page)

Sensory Activities

10. On Chart 8-B list five opportunities you saw which helped children learn through their senses.

Chart 8-B
LEARNING THROUGH THE SENSES

Opportunity	Experience that Took Place
Example: Water play	*Feeling the wetness of water.* *Seeing what floats and what sinks.* *Eye-to-hand coordination while pouring water from one container to another.* *Listening to the sound of water swishing inside containers when shaken.* *Measuring water in measuring cups.*
a.	
b.	

(Continued on next page)

Name _____ Date _____

(Play—continued)

Chart 8-B
LEARNING THROUGH THE SENSES Continued

Opportunity	Experience that Took Place
c.	
d.	
e.	

(Continued on next page)

EVALUATION:

1. How is play important to children's development?

2. Explain the meaning of the statement: Children learn through play.

3. Describe five examples of play and how they help a child develop.
   a.

   b.

(Play—continued)

c.

d.

e.

Chapter 9
Health and Safety

Children depend greatly on adults to provide them with safe and healthy places to live. Infants and toddlers are almost totally dependent on others for their safety and well-being. Even though the three to five year olds are gaining insight and grasping concepts about safety and health, they forget easily. They need lots of encouragement and reminders. Many young children become so involved in exciting activities that they forget to be careful.

The baby can be protected from harmful objects and hazardous surroundings easier than the toddler. This is because the baby cannot move about so easily. Obvious items can be kept out of sight and reach. Toddlers, however, are growing rapidly and become excited easily as they move about. They learn by doing. This means crawling and climbing into and on top of everything they can manage. Safety is no concern to them. This is also a difficult stage for safety because toddlers and adults do not adequately communicate yet. Toddlers do not understand the meaning of words such as poison, sharp, dangerous, and unsafe. Thus, adults must assume the responsibility of keeping the surroundings safe and healthy. They must always be alert to possible hazards in order to *prevent* accidents. Can you think of anything more agonizing than to wish you had been more alert? Any serious accident involving a young child is a tragedy.

As children approach the early years of three, four, and five, they learn quickly from models. They also learn by listening and talking. This is a good time to help them learn about safety. They are eager to please others. Often they will

Lifting children safely requires a firm but gentle grip.

Adults can assure safety while allowing children to do their own thing. Here, Lesa moved from sawing styrofoam to wood. Notice the organization of equipment that adds to the safety of this interest area.

Signs of a healthy child include clear skin, shiny hair, sparkling eyes, and a desire to explore and learn. Dennis passes the test.

Children have a natural desire to explore. They need the watchful eyes of adults nearby as they learn about the world around them.

enjoy following adult suggestions. Encouragement is meaningful to children at these ages. They like to know that adults have confidence in them. This is a stage in which children begin to develop habits of behavior. These habits influence them for life ahead. Their concept of self is built, to a great degree, upon how they interpret treatment from others. They quickly sense whether adults care enough about them to insure their safety.

Adults are responsible for seeing that all toys and equipment or materials for children's use are safe and free from any hazards. Children cannot always make sound judgments about their actions. They require adult help and limits to insure safety.

Whether at home or in community settings, sanitary conditions must prevail. Areas such as food preparation and service, toileting and bathing, and sleeping areas must be kept clean and safe. Of course, all play areas and surroundings, for all ages, should be constantly checked for cleanliness as well as safety.

Name _____ Date _____

Course _____ Experience # _____

HEALTHY CHILDREN

(To accompany Chapter 9)

OBJECTIVES:

- Describe the general behavior of a healthy child.
- Identify physical characteristics of a healthy child.

SETTING:

Type of situation (care center, family day care home, nursery, preschool, kindergarten, Head Start, private home, other) _____

Other information _____

Number of children present _____ Number of adults _____
Names and ages of children observed:

1. _____ Age _____

2. _____ Age _____

3. _____ Age _____

TASK:

Observe the same children several times and identify characteristics that indicate they are healthy. Use the following checklists to record your information.

Behavior

1. As you participate with children or observe them, notice their behavior. The healthy child usually behaves in positive and appropriate ways. On Chart 9-A check the items that are obvious.

Chart 9-A
BEHAVIOR OF A HEALTHY CHILD

	Yes	No	Not Sure
Cheerful.			
Appears to enjoy being with others.			
Copes with problems successfully most of the time.			
Likes to explore and try new ideas.			
Enjoys playing alone at times.			
Smiles or responds in positive ways to other children and adults.			
Attention span is long enough to enjoy interesting activities.			

(Continued on next page)

Physical Appearances

2. On Chart 9-B record information about the signs of general health by checking the items that are obvious. If you have some concern or question about one or more items, talk with the adult in charge. A child may need special attention.

Chart 9-B
SIGNS OF A HEALTHY CHILD

	Yes	No	Not Sure
Cheerful.			
Hair is glossy and clean.			
Eyes are bright and clear, without puffiness or redness.			
Absence of rash or splotches on skin, especially in tender areas.			
Lips are firm without cracks or blisters.			
Absence of lice in hair or on body.			
Skin tone is clear without paleness or extreme "yellowy" coloring.			
Tongue and gums appear firm without cracks, blisters. or bleeding.			
Throat is not swollen.			
Absence of sores on body.			
Simple cuts or bruises appear to be healing.			
Uses body with enthusiasm.			
Appears to have lots of energy.			
Rests when needed.			
Does not tire quickly with regular activities, including running and other active use of body.			
Likes to eat.			
Has a hearty appetite most of the time.			
Eats a variety of foods.			
Drinks milk and fruit and vegetable juices.			
Fingernails are firm without cracks around the cuticle.			
Does not bruise easily.			
Does not scratch or pick at body parts.			
Body temperature remains about the same.			
Shows enough strength for body size while playing with push, pull, lift, and carrying toys.			
Enjoys activities which require lots of body movement.			
Enjoys activities that are quiet in nature.			

(Continued on next page)

74

Name _____   Date _____

Chart 9-B
SIGNS OF A HEALTHY CHILD Continued

	Yes	No	Not Sure
Can sit for a while without getting frustrated or tense.			
Absence of cold or flu symptoms.			
Nose is not constantly dripping or runny.			
Throat is not sore or red.			
Ears are clear of liquid or excess wax.			
Child does not complain often about: Stomach hurting			
Ears aching			
Throat itching or hurting			
Legs or arms aching			
Teeth aching			
Other body parts			

EVALUATION:

1. Describe the expected behavior of a healthy child.

2. List ten physical characteristics of a healthy child.
   a.

   b.

(Continued on next page)

c.

d.

e.

f.

g.

h.

i.

j.

Name _____   Date _____

Course _____   Experience # _____

PROMOTING CHILDREN'S HEALTH

(*To accompany Chapter 9*)

OBJECTIVES:

- Plan activities that promote children's health.
- Identify routine experiences that help children develop sound health habits.

SETTING:

Type of situation (care center, family day care home, nursery, preschool, kindergarten, Head Start,

private home, other) _____

Number of children present _____   Number of adults _____
Names and ages of children observed:

1. _____   Age _____

2. _____   Age _____

3. _____   Age _____

Time of day _____

TASK:

Respond to the following items as you observe children or participate in their activities.

Children's Activities

Identify two children. Observe their participation in daily activities. Look for clues that indicate their health conditions. Describe what you observe about them in the following activities.

1. *Outdoor play* involving vigorous activities.

(Continued on next page)

2. *Individual, quiet type activities* such as puzzles, reading and listening, and manipulatives (eye-to-hand coordination required).

3. *Play activities requiring special physical and motor skills* such as sawing, hammering, block building, and cooking.

4. *Activities requiring concentration and problem solving* such as pouring liquids, measuring, and planting.

5. *Arts and creative media* in which children express their ideas and feelings through painting, working with clay and play dough, making collages, and cutting and pasting activities.

(Promoting Children's Health—continued)

Health Habits

6. What routine experiences do children have each day that help them develop sound health habits? On Chart 9-C record the evidence you see that children are learning about health.

Chart 9-C
DEVELOPING HEALTH HABITS

Behavior	What evidence did you see that children are learning about health?
Brushing teeth.	
Washing hands.	
Washing face.	
Eating healthy snacks (foods such as fruits, vegetables, simple bread and cereal products, and milk products).	
Eating balanced meals.	
Playing that requires use of: 　Large muscles.	
Body coordination.	
Eye-to-hand coordination.	
Use of the five senses.	
Toileting.	

(Continued on next page)

EVALUATION:

1. Discuss examples of how children's activities can promote health.

2. Explain how a daily routine can help children develop sound health habits.

Name _____   Date _____

Course _____   Experience # _____

SAFETY

(*To accompany Chapter 9*)

OBJECTIVES:

- Evaluate a children's setting for its safety.
- List basic safety features of toys, equipment, furnishings, rooms, and outdoor areas for children.
- Identify ways in which children learn safety for everyday living.

SETTING:

Type of situation (care center, family day care home, nursery, preschool, Head Start, kindergarten,

private home, other) _____

Other information _____

Number of children present _____   Number of adults _____
Names and ages of children observed:

1. _____ Age _____

2. _____ Age _____

3. _____ Age _____

Time of day _____

TASK:

Record your observations about safety for young children.

A Safe Setting

1. Whether in a home or community center, identify features of the environment that promoted safety for children. Check the items on the Chart 9-D checklist, marking the *yes* or *no* column depending on what you observe. If your response is *no,* give a brief explanation of what you found.

Chart 9-D
SAFETY CHECKLIST

Safety Features	Yes	No
Indoors		
Electrical outlets contained dummy plugs when not in use.		
No extension cords or electrical wires were hanging loose or in reach of children.		

(Continued on next page)

Chart 9-D

SAFETY CHECKLIST Continued

Safety Features	Yes	No
Furniture was well constructed and safe for use by children.		
Furniture was painted with non-toxic paint and was not peeling or cracking.		
Furniture was washable.		
Chairs, tables, and other furnishings were child size.		
Windows and screens were safely secured to prevent children from falling or crawling out.		
Door latches and locks were secure from children's reach and manipulative skills.		
Rugs were secure to prevent skidding and wrinkling that cause tripping.		
Toys and equipment were kept out of the traffic pattern to prevent falling and tripping.		
Toys and equipment were in safe working condition and easy for children to operate.		
Toys were painted with non-toxic paint that was not chipped or scraped.		
Tools and woodworking equipment for children's activities were kept in a safe place and in an organized manner.		

(Continued on next page)

(Safety—continued)

Chart 9-D
SAFETY CHECKLIST Continued

Safety Features	Yes	No
Blocks and large toys were stored in an organized way when not in use.		
Toilet areas were free of doors that would pinch little fingers.		
Toilet areas could be viewed by adults for the safety of the child during use.		
Toilet stools and wash basins were low enough for children to use with ease.		
Any steps used at basins or drinking fountains were wide and broad enough and strong enough to hold children securely.		
Hot water faucets for use by children had no leaks.		
Hot water temperature in children's sinks was not hot enough to burn a child's skin.		
Water spills were promptly mopped up to prevent slipping.		
Kitchen equipment was secure and out of children's reach or sight.		
Children were protected from handles and knobs on stoves and ranges.		
Tempting foods such as cookies were not stored in cabinets above such hazardous equipment as stoves, ranges, or sinks where exploring children might try to climb.		

(Continued on next page)

Chart 9-D
SAFETY CHECKLIST Continued

Safety Features	Yes	No
Outdoors Play area was free of all hazardous objects or garbage.		
A fence or wall prevented children from getting out of the designated play area.		
Children were supervised during walks and excursions outside of the play area.		
Tree limbs did not extend over hazardous objects or holes or pits in the ground.		
Toys and equipment were in safe working condition.		
Toys and equipment were painted with non-toxic paint and were not cracked or chipped.		
Toys and equipment were stored in a closed and locked area when not in use.		
Toys and equipment were not left in the traffic pattern of children.		
Small objects such as digging and sand play equipment were kept in designated areas near their place of use.		
Sand and water areas were securely covered when not in use.		
All children were in view of adults during outdoor play.		

(Safety—continued)

2. On Chart 9-E make a list of all dangerous or hazardous materials or substances that were in reach or view of children. (Examples are cleaning fluids, detergent, bleach, furniture polish, insect spray, and floor wax.)

Chart 9-E
SAFETY HAZARDS

List of Materials or Substances	Where Were These Located?
Example: Paint remover	*Under the kitchen sink*

Learning about Safety

3. What opportunities did children have to learn about safety through play? Answer by listing on Chart 9-F the kinds of activities that provided learning experiences. Also list what happened to indicate that children had an opportunity to learn.

Chart 9-F
LEARNING SAFETY THROUGH PLAY

Activity Areas and Play	Description of the Learning Experience
Dramatic play: Playing with dolls. Pretend cooking activities with stove.	*Example: Sheri was encouraged to place the doll baby in a low crib so it would not fall during sleep.*

(Continued on next page)

Chart 9-F
LEARNING SAFETY THROUGH PLAY Continued

Activity Areas and Play	Description of the Learning Experience
Blocks and large toys.	
Other: (list)	
Manipulative play: Stringing beads.	
Sewing or lacing.	
Pegs and boards.	
Other: (list)	
Carpentry area: Sawing wood.	
Hammering nails.	

(Continued on next page)

(Safety—continued)

Chart 9-F
LEARNING SAFETY THROUGH PLAY Continued

Activity Areas and Play	Description of the Learning Experience
Using a vice.	
Storing equipment.	
Other: (list)	
Science activities: Cooking experiences.	
Planting seeds and plants.	
Caring for plants.	
Feeding fish.	
Feeding pets.	
Weighing and measuring.	

(Continued on next page)

Chart 9-F
LEARNING SAFETY THROUGH PLAY Continued

Activity Areas and Play	Description of the Learning Experience
Water play.	
Sand play.	
Other: (list)	
Art and creative media: Use of paints.	
Pasting.	
Cutting.	
Playdough.	
Clay.	
Other: (list)	

(Continued on next page)

Name _____ Date _____

(Safety—continued)

LEARNING SAFETY THROUGH PLAY Continued

Activity Areas and Play	Description of the Learning Experience
Listening activities: Tape recorder and player. Head sets for listening. Other: (list)	

EVALUATION:

1. How does one determine the safety of a children's setting?

2. List two basic safety features for each of the following:
   a. Toys

   b. Play equipment such as tape recorders

(Continued on next page)

Copyright © 1977 by Henry E. Draper and Mary Wanda Draper

89

c. Children's furniture

d. The rooms in which children play

e. Outdoor play areas

3. Give three specific examples of how children can learn about safety through play.
   a.

   b.

   c.

Chapter 10
Building a Self-Concept

One of the most exciting things about human development is that each person is a unique individual. Each has special characteristics or features that belong only to that person. The *self* has a mind and a body that functions independently from all others. The self is made unique, however, by being in company with others. Without the presence of others, there would be no distinguishing personal characteristics.

Each child develops a *life-style.* This is one's unique or special way of behaving. This life-style adds to one's selfhood. It begins to take shape early in life. The life-style is influenced by what goes on around the child and how the child feels about the situation. By about the third year of life, most children are able to see themselves clearly as individuals. They see themselves as unique. They have their own identity. By this time the child has, to a great degree, laid the foundation for his or her life-style. The child's *autonomy* or selfhood is well underway. Autonomy brings about the need to be independent. Children begin to take on responsibility for their behavior and for many tasks of daily living.

You will see many examples of children showing their independence during play. They want to do things themselves without help from adults. This begins as early as during the first year of life. One of the first signs is when they become self-centered with the use of toys. Between about fifteen and twenty-one months of age, most children go through a negative stage. They let you know they have minds of their own. This is called *negativism.* It is to be expected of every child.

Children want and need attention from adults. They want to be recognized. They begin to see themselves as separate from others.

Children can draw their own conclusions about themselves when adults comment about the children's efforts and achievements.

Children need many positive experiences with parents in order to feel good about themselves.

Katherine enjoys doing things alone as well as with others. What does this tell you about her self-concept?

Gradually, children develop from being very self-centered to being able to share and respect feelings and needs of others. The better children feel about themselves, the easier it is to have respect for others. Children with positive thoughts about themselves are not easily threatened. They usually feel good about themselves without lots of special attention from others, that is, as long as they get an adequate amount of attention in everyday activities.

Children have unique ways of seeing and of thinking about themselves. Each child develops a *self-concept* or *self-image*. Several factors influence how children think about themselves. Examples include how others treat them and how each child interprets this treatment. This image is also influenced by how they see themselves within their surroundings. The picture they begin to form may be positive or it may be negative.

Children gradually learn what they are like in the eyes of others. This comes about as the child begins to understand how others feel and think. The way others respond to a child tells a lot about what they think of the child.

Children generally strive to live up to the image they have of themselves. Children who think of themselves as good, will usually behave in ways that reflect a positive self-concept. On the other hand, when self-worth is threatened often, children feel inferior. A different image may be revealed. These children may behave in ways that reflect negative self-concepts.

The child's health and general well-being also influences the self-concept. Handicaps, such as poor eyesight or inadequate hearing, may cause a child to feel inferior. Poor motor coordination, language disabilities, or physical defects often affect the child's view of self. A child with poor general health may reflect a feeling of inferiority.

Every child needs the support of others in order to build a positive self-image. Care, guidance, love, and encouragement help children feel secure. Children who receive lots of kind and warm responses from others usually develop positive self-images. Children who are punished severely or who are rejected may develop insecure feelings. They may develop negative pictures of themselves.

Success experiences help children think positively about themselves. Here are daily examples. When children are in control of their body movements during play, they feel successful. The use of language skills helps them relate to others. Success comes with taking care of such personal needs as toileting and eating. Making friends helps any child feel good.

You encourage children when they know that you have confidence in them. This is necessary as they face daily tasks. When children succeed, tell them what a good job they have done. When you talk with children, call them by name. This helps children see themselves as unique persons. They become important in the eyes of someone else. Provide enough success experiences to help each child feel adequate. Also provide enough challenging things for children to do so they will be encouraged to continue their efforts.

Children need time to play alone as well as with others. They need a place to retreat when they want to be alone. Children need time to themselves. They need privacy. They have thoughts and ideas that are their own.

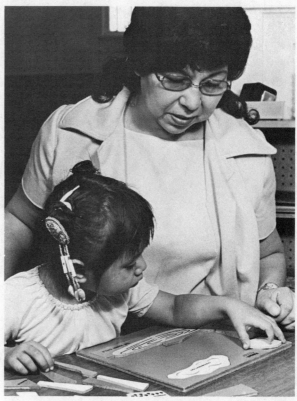

Care, guidance, love, and encouragement help children feel secure.

When children are in control of their body movements during play, they feel successful.

Let children know you have confidence in them. Billie Jo appears to feel secure as she pursues a puzzle.

One of the most exciting things about human development is that each person is a unique individual. The self is made unique, however, by being in company with others.

Name _____ Date _____

Course _____ Experience # _____

THE CHILD'S SELF-CONCEPT

(To accompany Chapter 10)

OBJECTIVES:
- Discuss the child's self-image and the influences that help shape it.
- Explain how the child draws conclusions about him- or herself as a result of everyday experiences.

SETTING:

Type of situation (care center, family day care home, nursery, preschool, kindergarten, Head Start,

private home, other) _____

Other information _____

Number of children present _____ Number of adults _____

Names and ages of children observed:

Girl _____ Age _____

Boy _____ Age _____

Time of day _____

TASK:

Follow one boy and one girl in their activities long enough to:
1. Record each one's encounters with adults and peers.

(Continued on next page)

2. Note the comments and non-verbal responses that each child receives.

3. Notice how each child responds to the comments and responses of others.

Name _____ Date _____

(The Child's Self-Concept—continued)

4. Check the list on Chart 10-A to indicate clues to how confident each child is about him- or herself.

Chart 10-A
CHECKLIST ON SELF-CONFIDENCE

Task	Boy	Girl
Takes own coat or jacket off with confidence.		
Takes care of own toileting needs without help from adult.		
Recognizes self in mirror and talks about self.		
Names own body parts.		
Face		
Eyes		
Chin		
Mouth		
Ears		
Cheeks		
Forehead		
Hair		
Chest		
Stomach		
Legs		
Feet		
Arms		
Hands		
Gives own name.		
Gives own address.		
Gives own telephone number.		
Knows names of brothers/sisters/parents.		
Recognizes photo of self.		
Makes comments that reflect confidence such as:		
"I can do it myself."		
"I know how to do that."		
"Let me do it."		

(Continued on next page)

EVALUATION:

1. How do others influence the child's self-image?

2. What can family members and adults do to help children develop positive self-concepts?

3. Give an example of an everyday experience which can affect a child's concept negatively or positively, depending upon how the adult responds to the child.

Chapter 11
Infancy

Infancy sets the stage for all of life to come. Immediately upon birth, the infant begins to interact with a new world. The infant is no longer in the safety of the *uterine environment,* the mother's uterus. Birth brings the infant into a world requiring many adjustments, both physical and social. The infant is no longer alone, but is in constant contact with others. Those who provide care and love to meet everyday needs become the most important persons in the infant's life.

The infant is dependent on others for physical needs such as toileting, feeding, clothing, and sleeping. Protection from hazardous surroundings is the adult's responsibility. Tender loving care, with consistency, is needed from those closest to the new baby. Trust begins to develop as daily needs are met in a pleasant and relaxed atmosphere. Comfort and security emerge as the infant experiences many positive responses from others. The family becomes the most important influence on the infant's development.

The infant constantly receives stimulation through the senses. This occurs as the baby moves about and through body contact with objects and people. The infant gradually becomes a coordinated person. At first, movements are random and without purpose. Later, the infant gains control over body parts and begins to move with a purpose. For example, the very young baby grasps anything that comes into contact with the hands. Later, after a few months, the baby follows an object with the eyes and tries to grasp it with the hands.

As we study the infant, there are many clues that help us see where the infant is in the developmental process. For example, before about nine months of age, the infant does not know that objects are permanent. When the object is

Close contact and lots of loving care help infants become secure and happy individuals. Parents have the responsibility of helping infants develop trust. They must also help their children extend this trust to others.

Baby Elizabeth sees the ball and reaches for it. Notice the mother is saying "ball" as she plays with the baby.

out of sight, it is "out of mind." When Mother walks out of the room, the baby thinks she no longer exists. The infant has not yet developed *object permanence.* The baby will not look for the "lost" person or object. This is because the infant's memory has not developed adequately by this age. The infant's memory improves greatly by about ten to twelve months of age. You will see the child looking in the place where an object was last played with or seen (such as a ball under a chair). Now you know the child is grasping *object permanency.* Can you see how this ability changes the infant's perspective on life?

Infants, during about the first year, must manipulate objects in order to solve problems. For example, Jeremy, age twelve months, had been playing with a colorful stacking tower. It contained plastic rings of graduated sizes. He placed them on the tower by trial and error until he finally stacked them correctly. Then, at about age fourteen months, Jeremy's mother noticed that he never made a mistake in placing the rings on the tower in the correct order. She observed this several times. What has hap-

pened to Jeremy? He has developed the ability to manipulate the objects mentally. He no longer has to use the method of manually trying out each ring for the tower. He can remember that each ring is a different size.

During late infancy, the child gradually plays with toys with a purpose in mind. Consider these examples. Erik rolled the ball to get it to his dad. Maria pulled the ring on a string to get it close to her body. Leah pulled the string on her musical toy to hear the jingling bell ring.

As you can see, infancy is an exciting period. It is constantly filled with rapid development. Both the body and the mind are growing and maturing. Infants quickly outgrow their clothing. They need simple designs in clothes that allow them to move all body parts with ease. Infants need to be able to scoot and roll and crawl. They need practice to get around by their own body control as much as possible.

The five senses are needed to provide information about the child's world. Infants need lots of colorful objects that are easily seen and safely constructed. Also, they should be out of the playpen as much as possible. They need

The experiences Amy had during infancy set the stage for her continued development of the senses.

How exciting it is to have parents nearby to share in playful activities. Can you see why Dennis is such a happy child?

room to explore and discover all of their surroundings.

Even though infants cannot talk, it is not too early to start talking to them. You can sing songs, say rhymes, and talk to the baby. Do this as diapers are changed, during the bathing process, and at feeding times. Whenever an adult is near the infant, some talking is usually helpful. Soft voices have a soothing effect that comforts and pleases the baby. Language be-

gins as others talk to the baby. Even when babies cannot respond with words, they become acquainted with sounds and voices. What could be a better way to help the infant begin the development of a positive self-concept? The infant needs to consistently hear kindly spoken words with expressions of warmth and caring. Positive feelings begin this way. This sets the stage for all of life to come.

Name _____   Date _____

Course _____   Experience # _____

INFANCY: FIRST THREE MONTHS

(To accompany Chapter 11)

OBJECTIVES:

- Explain the infant's need for adult care and attention during the first three months of life.
- Discuss the influence of parents and other adults on the infant's behavior:
- Describe typical sleeping patterns during early infancy.

SETTING:

Type of situation (care center, family day care home, kindergarten, Head Start, nursery, preschool, private home, other) _____

Other information _____

Number of children present _____ Number of adults _____

Names and ages of children observed:

1. _____ Age _____

2. _____ Age _____

3. _____ Age _____

Time of day _____

TASK:

As you care for, or observe another person caring for, an infant (birth to three months) respond to the following items.

Comforting

1. When the infant was upset, which of the following procedures were used to help the infant settle?

  a. Talking to the infant? Yes _____ If not, what was done?

  b. Placing adult hand on the infant's belly and holding one or both of the infant's arms? Yes _____ If not, what was done?

  c. Restraining the infant with force? Yes _____ If not, what was done?

(Continued on next page)

d. Holding and cuddling the infant? Yes _____ If not, what was done?

e. Rocking the infant by holding gently in adult's lap and arms? Yes _____ If not, what was done?

Which of the procedures recorded would you have used?

Why?

Response to Toys

2. Using a simple auditory toy (toy that makes sound), place it in hearing range of the infant and cause it to make a sound. What was the infant's response to the *auditory* toy?

a. Infant turned head toward place where sound came from. Yes _____ No _____
b. Showed alertness but did not attempt to locate the source of sound.

Yes _____ No _____
c. The infant showed no reaction. _____

3. Using a visual toy (toy that appeals to child's sight), place it in viewing range of the child. What was the infant's response to the *visual* toy?
a. Infant focused on the toy and followed it with eyes and head moving back and forth.

Yes _____ No _____
b. Infant focused on toy and followed with both eyes but did not turn head.

Yes _____ No _____
c. Infant focused on toy when it was presented but showed little interest.

Yes _____ No _____

d. Did not follow movement of toy with eyes. _____

e. Did not focus or follow toy with eyes. _____

Response to Persons

4. Observe an infant when a familiar adult is close by and talking to the infant. What was the infant's response to stimulation from the adult (such as the adult looking at baby and smiling, singing, or cuddling)? Respond by answering the following:

a. Infant turned head toward place where sound came from. Yes _____ No _____

b. Infant showed alertness but did not attempt to locate the source of sound.

Yes _____ No _____

(Infancy: First Three Months—continued)

   c. Infant focused on the person and followed that person with eyes and head moving back and forth. Yes _____ No _____

   d. Infant focused on the person and followed with both eyes but did not turn head. Yes _____ No _____

   e. Infant focused on person but showed little interest. Did not follow with eyes. _____

   f. Did not focus or follow person with eyes. _____

   g. Infant showed no reaction. _____

Sleeping

5. How did the infant respond while sleeping in a *deep sleep* state?

   a. Regular breathing was evident. Yes _____ No _____

   b. Eyes were closed. Yes _____ No _____

   c. Spontaneous activity was obvious. Yes _____ No _____

6. How did the infant respond while sleeping in a *light sleep* state?

   a. Eyes remained closed. Yes _____ No _____

   b. Eye movement occurred under the closed eyelid. Yes _____ No _____

   c. Low activity included random movements and startled movements. Yes _____ No _____

   d. Breathing was sometimes irregular. Yes _____ No _____

   e. Sucking movements occurred off and on. Yes _____ No _____

Awakened State

7. Drowsy or semi-dozing

   a. Eyes were open. Yes _____ No _____

   b. Eyes were fluttering. Yes _____ No _____

   c. Mildly startled from time to time. Yes _____ No _____

   d. Activity level was varied—some quiet periods and some movements. Yes _____ No _____

8. Alert and awake

   a. Had bright alert look. Yes _____ No _____

   b. Seemed to focus attention on people or other objects. Yes _____ No _____

   c. Showed body activity with thrusting movements. Yes _____ No _____

   d. Snuggled with a low activity rate. Yes _____ No _____

   e. Crying was intense. Yes _____ No _____

   f. Gentle, soft crying occurred. Yes _____ No _____

(Continued on next page)

Cuddling Behavior

9. How did the infant respond to being held when placed in a cuddling position against the adult's chest and shoulder?

    a. Lay against the adult and relaxed? Yes _____ No _____ Rested head on shoulder and neck or elbow of the adult? Yes _____ No _____

    b. Did not resist being held but did not participate with nestling responses; lay passively in arms and against the shoulder of adult (like a sack of flour)? Yes _____ No _____

    c. Actually resisted being held, continually pushed away—became stiffened?

    Yes _____ No _____

EVALUATION:

1. Why is it so important for adults to provide care and attention to the infant during the first three months of life?

2. Explain how parents and other close adults influence the infant's behavior.

3. Give examples of several typical sleeping patterns during early infancy.

106

Name _____ Date _____

Course _____ Experience # _____

INFANCY: FIRST SIX MONTHS

(To accompany Chapter 11)

OBJECTIVES:
- Describe the infant's ability to respond to objects during the first six months of life.
- Explain the term "tracking" and its importance during early infancy.

SETTING:

Type of situation (care center, family day care home, nursery, preschool, kindergarten, Head Start,

private home, other)_____

Other information _____

Number of children present _____ Number of adults _____
Names and ages of children observed:

1. _____ Age _____

2. _____ Age _____

3. _____ Age _____

Time of day _____

TASK:

Observe an infant age one to six months. Notice how the senses and body work (sensorimotor characteristics) together for the baby. Record your findings.

Reflex Action

1. Place an object so that it touches the palm of the infant's hand. (Place your finger or a rattle in the infant's hand.)
   What did the baby do?

   a. Grasped the object tightly? Yes _____ No _____

   b. Baby moved hand away from object? Yes _____ No _____

   c. Baby did nothing at all. _____

   d. Comments:

(Continued on next page)

Coordinated Movements

Coordinated movements include the following:

SEEING AND GRASPING

2. Place an object such as a fuzzy ball within the baby's easy reach and in line of the baby's vision.

What did the baby do?

    a. Looked at object and grasped it? Yes _____ No _____

    b. Grasped object without looking at it? Yes _____ No _____

    c. Baby did nothing at all. _____

    Comments:

HEARING AND GRASPING

3. Place an object such as a rattle or a squeeze toy within the baby's easy reach and make a sound with the toy that the baby can hear.

What did the baby do?

    a. Turned head toward source of sound and reached to grasp object?

Yes _____ No _____

    b. Reached for object after seeing it, but did not seem to hear sound?

Yes _____ No _____

    c. Baby did nothing at all. _____

    Comments:

TRACKING

4. Place a colorful mobile or object over an infant's crib or bed. Place it to the left or right side of the crib. Watch the infant's eye and body movements. Describe what the infant did.

(Infancy: First Six Months—continued)

5. Place the infant on your lap or on a parent's or adult's lap. Move your arm and hand back and forth slowly in line of the baby's vision. Watch the baby's eye movements. Did the infant show

evidence of tracking—following the movement with the eyes? Yes _____   No _____
Describe what happened.

EVALUATION:

1. Discuss the infant's progress from reflex action to coordinated movements during the first six months of life.

2. Give two examples of the infant's ability to track objects by eye movements. What is the importance of tracking in early development?

Name _____   Date _____

Course _____   Experience # _____

INFANCY: SEVEN TO EIGHTEEN MONTHS

(To accompany Chapter 11)

OBJECTIVES:
- Describe how the infant uses the five senses in activities with play objects.
- Describe how the infant uses the body in activities with play objects.
- Identify characteristics of the infant that reflect the need for sensory or motor actions.

SETTING:

Type of situation (care center, nursery, preschool, family day care home, Head Start, kindergarten,

private home, other) _____

Other information _____

Number of children present _____   Number of adults _____

Names and ages of children observed:

1. _____   Age _____

2. _____   Age _____

3. _____   Age _____

Time of day _____

TASK:

Observe an infant about age seven to eighteen months. Record actions of the infant for each of the following:

Pushing-Pulling

1. With the infant in a sitting position, place a push-pull toy in front of infant about eighteen inches away. Sit or stand behind the infant and pull the string of the toy to pull the toy toward the child until the child can grasp it. What did the child do?

(Continued on next page)

Did the child replace the toy at a distance? Yes _____ No _____ Replace the toy at eighteen inches away and pull it again toward the child. Did the infant attempt to imitate by pulling the string? Yes _____ No _____ Describe what happened.

2. Place a push-pull toy in close range of child. With no modeling or helping, observe what the child does with the toy. Describe what happened.

Modeling

3. Tie a colorful ribbon or yarn (twelve to eighteen inches long) around a plastic ring or jar lid ring (about three to four inches in diameter). Pull the ring by the string so the infant can see you. Repeat this a few times. Let the infant play with the object. Describe the infant's activity.

Object Permanence

4. Use an object (a ball or small toy such as a teddy bear) during play with the infant. After a few minutes of play, place an opaque cloth (a cloth through which you cannot see) over the object. Did the infant look for the object under the cloth? Yes _____ No _____ What did the infant do?

(Infancy: Seven to Eighteen Months—continued)

Repetitious Sounds

5. Sing a simple song or play pat-a-cake with the infant. Describe the infant's response.

If the child did not respond to the singing or pat-a-cake, use a toy that rings when shaken. Shake it for the child. Give it to the child. Did the child repeat the sound of the bell by shaking the object?

Yes _____ No _____ Describe the infant's activity.

Sensorimotor Activity

6. Place a toy such as a stacking tower in front of the infant. Let the infant play with the object. Describe the infant's actions.

EVALUATION:

1. Describe how the infant uses the senses during play.

2. Describe how the infant uses body movements during play.

(Continued on next page)

3. List four characteristics of the infant that reflect the need for sensory and motor activities.

a.

b.

c.

d.

Chapter 12

Motor Development and Coordination

Motor development includes the child's increasing ability to control body parts and body movements. From numerous studies made of infants and young children, the following facts about motor development emerge:

- Development of muscle control depends upon the maturation of the neural structures, bones and muscles, and changes in body proportions.
- Learning and control cannot occur until maturation has laid the groundwork.
- Motor development follows a predictable pattern.
- There are predictable stages within the pattern of motor development.
- There are individual differences in the rate of motor development.

As children progress in motor skills, they are able to enjoy a great variety of activities. Some require coordination of *gross* or large muscles and others require coordination of *fine* or small muscles. Examples of gross motor activities include the use of the whole body such as rolling, running, and climbing. Examples of fine motor activities include the use of eye-to-hand coordination such as in putting puzzles together, stringing beads, and hammering nails.

Young children learn more about their world as they use their bodies and minds together. They learn as they explore and investigate, as they move about, and as they express themselves.

Observing children's involvement in all types of activities over a long period of time is helpful. You will gradually become acquainted with each child's level of motor ability. The *Inventory of Motor Skills* is to be used as a guide. It will help you increase your knowledge about levels of motor development. Of course, this technique, alone, will not tell you all you need to know about a child's motor skills.

Adults can introduce new materials and equipment to children that help develop large and small muscle control.

Large muscles and body control are exercised as Nathan enjoys outdoor activities.

Ryan and Tony enjoy table activities involving eye-to-hand coordination as well as concept formation.

Lesa uses her skills in eye-to-hand coordination as she strings macaroni to make a necklace.

As you look over the inventory, you will notice the age ranges on the left include some expected motor tasks. As you observe a child, you must decide what age range is most appropriate. Keep in mind that although all children go through the same steps or sequence of development, each progresses at an individual rate. Some are slower and some are faster than others. For example, you may observe a child seventeen to thirty months of age who can also perform tasks listed for the fourteen- to seventeen-month-old or the twenty-four- to thirty-six-month-old child. In such a case, check all the tasks you actually observe the child doing. This will help identify the level of that particular child's development.

Remember, the same child may do well in a task one day and not so well the next, depending on how the day goes. You will have the best results by making at least two or three observations on two or three different days to watch the same child.

Name _____ Date _____

Course _____ Experience # _____

MOTOR DEVELOPMENT

(To accompany Chapter 12)

OBJECTIVES:

- Define motor development.
- Identify levels of specific motor skills in young children.
- Describe examples of the step-by-step sequence by which children develop motor skills.
- Explain the value of knowing how young children develop in a step-by-step process.

SETTING:

Type of situation (care center, family day care home, nursery, preschool, kindergarten, Head Start,

private home, other) _____

Other information _____

Number of children present _____ Number of adults _____
Names and ages of children observed:

1. _____ Age _____

2. _____ Age _____

3. _____ Age _____

4. _____ Age _____

Date of Trial I _____ Date of Trial II _____ Date of Trial III _____

TASK:

Identify one child at each stage of development (infant, toddler, romper, kindergartner) and check the trial columns on Chart 12-A to indicate which motor skills each child has mastered. This checklist may require several observations to complete each trial.

Chart 12-A
INVENTORY OF MOTOR SKILLS

Record the date under the trial column to indicate when the inventory was used. Place a check mark in the trial column to indicate which motor skills the child has mastered. Be certain the child has repeated the skill so that you are not simply observing a coincidence. Waiting a few months between trials will help you see the child's progress.

INFANT

	Trial I	Trial II	Trial III
Name of Child_____ Age_____ Date of Each Trial:			
Birth to 3 Months Lifts head when held at shoulder.			
Smiles spontaneously.			

(Continued on next page)

Chart 12-A
INVENTORY OF MOTOR SKILLS Continued
INFANT

	Trial I	Trial II	Trial III
Name of Child_____ Age_____ Date of Each Trial:			
Turns head to hear speaking voices.			
Responds to bell or rattle.			
Follows moving person.			
Follows objects 180° (along a straight line).			
Makes pushing movements with arms and legs when held.			
3 to 5 Months Smiles in response to others or objects.			
Rolls over.			
In sitting position head is erect and steady.			
Smiles at mirror image.			
Both hands approach offered object (bell or rattle).			
Crawling movements begin.			
5 to 9 Months Transfers object from hand to hand.			
Sits without support.			
Squeals with joy or pleasure.			
Reaches and grasps toy.			
Holds two small toys or two cubes.			
6 to 12 Months Crawls or moves on stomach or hitches in sitting position, progresses without walking.			
Gets to sitting position alone.			
Exhibits thumb-finger grasp.			
Feeds self a cracker.			
Imitates speech sounds of others.			
Stands by holding on to something.			
9 to 15 Months Cooperates in playing pat-a-cake.			
Walks, holding on to furniture.			
Stands alone.			
Looks at pictures in baby picture book.			

(Continued on next page)

Name _____ Date _____

(Motor Development—continued)

Chart 12-A
INVENTORY OF MOTOR SKILLS Continued
INFANT

	Trial I	Trial II	Trial III
Name of Child _____			
Age _____ Date of Each Trial:			
11 to 15 Months Walks alone, toddling.			
Neat pincer grasp, as picking up raisin.			
Indicates or gestures what is wanted without crying.			
Drinks from cup.			
12 to 18 Months Turns pages of a book.			
Builds tower of two cubes.			
Scribbles spontaneously.			

TODDLER

	Trial I	Trial II	Trial III
18 to 22 Months Removes simple garment.			
Walks backward.			
Builds tower of three cubes.			
Walks up steps with help.			
Carries and hugs doll or stuffed animal.			
14 to 17 Months Throws ball overhand.			
Runs.			
Uses spoon, spills some food.			
Points to parts of doll.			
17 to 30 Months Walks up steps alone.			
Recognizes and points to five pictures.			
24 to 36 Months Walks backward.			
Walks up steps with help but not on all fours.			
Climbs on furniture, stairs, obstacles.			
Kicks ball forward.			

(Continued on next page)

Chart 12-A
INVENTORY OF MOTOR SKILLS Continued
TODDLER

	Trial I	Trial II	Trial III
Name of Child_____ Age_____ Date of Each Trial:			
24 to 36 Months Throws ball overhand, not directed in aim.			
Runs.			
Builds tower of three or more cubes.			
Unwraps, removes covers from candy, gum, or other objects.			
Peels bananas.			
Disassembles; takes simple objects apart with minimal difficulty.			
Unfastens clothing.			
ROMPER			
36 to 48 Months Marches to rhythm.			
Runs, jumps, hops, skips, gallops.			
Climbs stairs and descends stairs.			
Slides in skating and dancing motion.			
Rolls and crawls on the floor.			
Balances on one foot.			
Kicks a ball.			
Jumps over a rope.			
Pedals (tricycle; bicycle).			
Touches toes with hands from a standing position.			
Does sit-ups.			
Does chin-ups.			
Does push-ups.			
Throws and bounces a ball.			
Catches a ball or a bean bag.			
Pulls and pushes objects.			
Strings beads.			
Cuts with scissors.			
Uses large crayons and pencils.			

(Continued on next page)

Chart 12-A
INVENTORY OF MOTOR SKILLS Continued
ROMPER

	Trial I	Trial II	Trial III
Name of Child _____			
Age _____ Date of Each Trial:			
36 to 48 Months Rolls wrists and closes fists.			
Cuts out assorted shapes with scissors.			
Folds paper.			
Builds with blocks.			
Unscrews and screws objects.			
Scribbles.			
Draws directed lines.			
Can do manipulative puzzles.			
Takes simple objects apart.			
Puts simple parts together that require little mechanical skill.			
Puts simple objects together.			
Uses simple building blocks, color blocks, construction toys; shows imagination.			
Draws a circle, usually from a copy.			
Builds a tower of eight or more cubes.			
Takes one step per tread when climbing.			
Stands on one foot for one second.			
KINDERGARTNER			
48 to 60 Months Throws ball overhand (distance, direction, and accuracy not essential).			
Catches and throws 12″ ball.			
Catches and throws 5″ ball.			
Catches and throws 3″ ball.			
Bounces and catches balls of varying sizes.			
Can climb equipment (jungle gym, etc).			
Balances on one foot for one second.			

(Continued on next page)

Chart 12-A
INVENTORY OF MOTOR SKILLS Continued
KINDERGARTNER

	Trial I	Trial II	Trial III
Name of Child_____			
Age_____ Date of Each Trial:			
48 to 60 Months			
Hops on both feet.			
Hops on one foot.			
Hops on one foot—four steps.			
Is learning to skip.			
Skips in unison to music.			
Skips rope.			
Balances on balancing beam.			
Buttons buttons.			
Zips zippers.			
Ties simple bow.			
Threads beads or spools on string.			
Plays jacks.			
Pounds and rolls clay or playdough.			
Forms crude objects with clay.			
Creates recognizable objects with clay.			
Places blocks horizontally on floor.			
Stacks blocks vertically.			
Creates recognizable structures with blocks.			
Participates in finger plays.			
Understands use of scissors.			
Cuts and pastes according to directions.			
Cuts and pastes creative designs.			
Maintains rhythmic beat with rhythm instruments.			
Participates in square dancing.			
Places pegs on pegboard without a pattern.			
Places pegs on pegboard forming a design.			
Builds structures with tinker toys or Lincoln logs.			
Participates vigorously in outdoor play.			
Climbs adeptly on jungle gym, without difficulty.			
Rides tricycle with speed and skill.			

(Continued on next page)

Name _____ Date _____

(Motor Development—continued)

Chart 12-A
INVENTORY OF MOTOR SKILLS Continued
KINDERGARTNER

	Trial I	Trial II	Trial III
Name of Child _____ Age _____ Date of Each Trial: ____			
48 to 60 Months Shows interest in woodworking materials.			
Attempts to use hammers and saws.			
Hammers with some dexterity.			
Saws with some dexterity.			
Produces unidentifiable art work.			
Produces recognizable art projects.			
Pours from small pitcher into glass.			
Holds and eats with spoon or fork correctly.			
Uses knife to cut food or spread butter, etc.			
Joins in games (such as "Drop the Hanky," "Skip to My Lou," "Farmer in the Dell").			
Turns about in small circles as in dancing.			
Hops on one foot, then the other.			
Skips in continuous movement from place to place.			
Hammers nails into a board until they are secure.			

EVALUATION:

1. Define motor development.

(Continued on next page)

2. Give examples of several levels of the same motor skill.

3. Why is it important for parents and persons who work with children to have knowledge about the step-by-step process of development?

Name _____ Date _____

Course _____ Experience # _____

MOTOR COORDINATION
(*To accompany Chapter 12*)

OBJECTIVES:
- Define and describe motor coordination in young children.
- Discuss the difference in *gross* and *fine* motor control.
- Explain how motor coordination affects a child's self-concept.

SETTING:

Type of situation (care center, family day care home, nursery or preschool, kindergarten, private

home, Head Start, other) _____

Other information _____

Number of children present _____ Number of adults _____
Names and ages of children observed:

1. _____ Age _____

2. _____ Age _____

3. _____ Age _____

Time of day _____

TASK:

Look for examples of motor activity and children's development of control over various muscles and body parts. Record your observations.

Motor Coordination

1. Observe three children. Describe evidence of each one's level of motor coordination for the tasks listed on Chart 12-B.

Chart 12-B
DEVELOPING MOTOR COORDINATION

Task	Child I	Child II	Child III
Example: Snapping garment.	Used both hands.	Could not snap.	Tried three times and asked for help.
a. Buttoning or zipping garments.			

(Continued on next page)

Chart 12-B
DEVELOPING MOTOR COORDINATION Continued

Task	Child I	Child II	Child III
b. Washing and drying hands.			
c. Taking off clothing.			
d. Putting on clothing.			
e. Manipulating toys.			
f. Meeting own toileting needs.			

(Motor Coordination—continued)

2. Observe two children as they play. What examples of gross motor skills did you see? What examples of fine motor skills did you see? On Chart 12-C identify the activities in which children were involved while you observed these areas of development.

Chart 12-C
GROSS AND FINE MOTOR SKILLS

Gross Motor Skills	Child I	Child II
Activities:	Skills:	Skills:
Example: Pushing a large barrel.	Child used entire body with arms extended to push barrel.	Child placed chest against barrel and pushed with whole body.

(Continued on next page)

Chart 12-C
GROSS AND FINE MOTOR SKILLS Continued

Fine Motor Skills	Child I	Child II
Activities:	Skills:	Skills:
Example: *Hammering nails into styrofoam.*	*Child pushed nails into styrofoam to secure it, then hit it with a hammer until all the way in. Eye-to-hand coordination was good.*	

(Motor Coordination—continued)

3. In a group of boys and girls in the same age range, did you notice any differences in motor skills? If so, explain and give examples. If you did not notice any difference, explain what they did that was the same.

4. What specific skills did you observe that showed children's control of leg muscles and movements? What was the child's response—either verbal or non-verbal, about the activity?

(Continued on next page)

5. What types of awkwardness did you observe? In your opinion, what appeared to be the main causes of each situation? What did the child do or say in each situation?

6. What specific skills did you observe in a child's control of:
   a. Arm muscles.

   b. Eye-to-hand coordination.

7. What difficulties did you see children having in Number 6? What do you think contributes to the difficulty in each case?

EVALUATION:

1. List ten activities which promote a child's motor coordination. Identify each activity as requiring *gross* or *fine* motor control.
   a.

   b.

(Motor Coordination—continued)

    c.

    d.

    e.

    f.

    g.

    h.

    i.

    j.

2. What is the relationship between motor coordination and the child's self-concept?

Chapter 13
Intellectual Development

Although children go through the same pattern and sequence of development, each progresses at an individual rate and in a unique way. According to the Swiss psychologist Jean Piaget, three major factors influence the child's intellectual development:

1. Maturation—the mind matures in order for a child to increase thinking skills just as muscles and bones mature in order for a child to increase body coordination.

2. Experience—the active involvement in everyday living. This includes people, places, and things.

3. Social transmission—the communication of knowledge and ideas by other human beings.

As you study the intellectual development of young children, you begin to see how they think by observing their actions and responses. Keep these points in mind:

• Children learn best by interacting with things and people around them.

• Children have a natural desire to explore and experiment. They are curious.

• They learn by asking questions when they are interested and by listening to what others are saying.

Young children, up to about age seven, have a logic of their own. *They believe what they see.* Even when an object such as a playdough ball is transformed into a new shape, they do not understand that the volume or amount of playdough remains the same. In other words, they cannot understand that the substance can be *returned* to the original shape. They cannot *reverse* a process of the mind.

Children up to about six or seven years of age are *egocentric.* This means each child thinks from his or her own point of view. The child cannot see the situation from someone else's position.

Notice how children still use their bodies to help solve problems. Watch children cut with scissors. Notice how they open and shut their mouths. Notice how they move their shoulders and their arms.

Children develop concepts, or ideas and notions, about objects and the world by getting involved. For example, Ora grasps the idea of what *up* means when she climbs on top of a box or climbing gym. She gets the idea of *under* when she hides beneath the table. Doing the action with her body means more than looking at a picture or hearing someone talk about these concepts.

Adapted from the theory of Jean Piaget is the notion that children generally represent the real world at four levels. They progress from the lowest to the highest level with maturation, experience, and social contacts. The four levels include:

As Lesa cares for plants that she and her playmates planted, she experiences ideas about the passage of time as well as about plants. She actually sees the results of growth and development of plants taking place over a period of time.

John is curious about the fish in their environment. He wants to know about the plants and shells, too.

Notice how children get involved with their activities. A child's mouth often reflects the child's efforts at accomplishing a task or solving a problem.

Dramatic play provides many opportunities for children to enjoy playing roles of family members. Thinking skills and problem-solving techniques develop along with fine motor skills.

1. *Object Level*—Learning about the real thing by interacting with the real object. For example, Janet learns about the telephone by touching it, dialing, listening to someone talk through it, listening to the ring, and seeing others actually use it.

2. *Index Level*—The second level is called the *index* of the real object. This level requires the use of one or more of the five senses. Either some part of the real thing or a sound, smell, or taste from it alerts the child to what the real object is. For example, the child hears the telephone ringing. The child who has had lots of object experiences with the real telephone does not have to see it to know that the ring *refers to* the telephone.

3. *Symbol Level*—Only after the child has had ample experience at the object and index levels will that child use symbols. Only then will the child be able to represent the real object with a symbol such as a picture. The picture is *not* the real thing and there is no sound, smell, or taste coming from it. But often after adequate experience at both the object and index levels, the child will recognize a *picture.* The child recognizes the picture of the telephone and knows that it represents the real thing. The adult world is full of symbols. It is easy to assume that children can use pictures and other symbols such as television, and drawings to represent the real things. Observe children closely and you will see that they do not always see pictures as adults do. A *hat* may look like a *cap* to a child, or a *bat* may look like a stick. A drawing of a round face may look like a cookie. Only after we know children understand the object and index levels can we expect them to represent reality by the use of symbols.

4. *Sign Level*—This fourth level is the use of a *sign* such as a word to represent the real thing. The word *telephone* will mean little to a child who does not know how to read. Many children learn their own names—*signs* which refer to *them.* Even though they cannot read, many young children begin to recognize signs if they have lots of experience with them. Have you ever heard a mother say to the father in front of the young child, "We will have c-o-o-k-i-e-s (spells it aloud) after lunch." And the child says, "Mother, can I have a cookie now?" They have heard this *sign* used enough to know what it refers to even though they cannot see, touch, smell, or taste the cookies.

We do not have to *teach* children colors, numbers, or letters. They learn these concepts by playing with objects. They learn labels by listening to others talking in everyday experiences. As a child picks up a blue triangle, the adult might simply say, "You picked up a blue triangle," or, "Another blue triangle." Eventually a child will grasp the idea and it will have meaning. But we do not always help children by quizzing them or by asking them lots of questions such as "What color is this?" "What shape is that?" "How many blocks do you have?" If you know the child knows the colors, shapes, and numbers, you may wish to ask, however. In this way you may give the child an opportunity to respond with success. However, this does not always insure learning.

Children's behavior depends greatly on how they think. Their actions give you clues to their intellectual abilities. They have their own reasons for their actions. As you observe them you begin to see these reasons.

Name _____   Date _____

Course_____   Experience # _____

UNDERSTANDING INTELLECTUAL DEVELOPMENT

(To accompany Chapter 13)

OBJECTIVES:
- Describe the process of intellectual development during the early years of childhood.
- Cite examples of how children solve problems in daily living.
- Discuss how intellectual development is stimulated during the preschool years.

SETTING:

Type of situation (care center, nursery or preschool, kindergarten, family day care home, Head

Start, private home, other) _____

Other information _____

Number of children present _____   Number of adults _____

Name of child observed: _____   Age: _____

Time of day _____

TASK:

Observe one child and respond to the items below.

Thinking

1. List four examples that indicated the child was thinking about what was going on.
   a.

   b.

   c.

   d.

Forming Ideas

2. What did the child do that reflects the ability to form concepts, or ideas, about the following?
   a. Shape

(Continued on next page)

b. Color

c. Size

d. Space

e. Weight

f. Numbers

g. Time

h. Seriation, or ordering

i. Classification, or grouping

j. Self-image

Learning through Play

3. Give two examples of what the child appeared to have learned during play.

a.

b.

(Understanding Intellectual Development—continued)

Problem Solving

4. How did each interest area in the room contribute to the child's ability to solve problems? (Notice the example on Chart 13-A.)

Chart 13-A
SOLVING PROBLEMS IN INTEREST AREAS

Interest Area	Problem	What Happened?
Example: *Science area*	*How to get the fish food in the can behind the fish tank.*	*John moved away objects on the wide (24") window sill next to the fish tank. He boosted himself up so that he balanced himself with his tummy on the edge of the sill while reaching behind the tank for the can of fish food. After feeding the fish, he returned the can in the same manner. Then he replaced the objects next to the tank. Storing the can behind the tank provided a problem-solving situation.*

(Continued on next page)

Chart 13-A

SOLVING PROBLEMS IN INTEREST AREAS Continued

Interest Area	Problem	What Happened?

Trial and Error

5. Describe two examples of how the child solved a problem by trial and error. *EXAMPLE: Sally manipulated the cubes with her hands until they fit into the slots of corresponding sizes.*

   a.

   b.

Active Learning

6. Give three examples of how the child used his or her body while solving a problem. *EXAMPLE: The child's mouth opened wide when trying to put an object, by hand, into a small opening in a box.*

   a.

   b.

   c.

EVALUATION:

1. *Development is sequential.*
Describe two activities that are examples of how learning takes place in a step-by-step process.

   a.

   b.

(Continued on next page)

2. *Learning progresses from simple to complex levels.*
Describe how children begin to formulate concepts at a very simple level of learning with *real objects* and gradually progress to more difficult levels of abstract thinking.

3. *Promoting intellectual development.*
As a result of your involvement with children, recommend four ways to promote intellectual development during the preschool years.

a.

b.

c.

d.

Name _____   Date _____

Course _____   Experience # _____

CONCEPT FORMATION

(To accompany Chapter 13)

OBJECTIVES:

- Illustrate, with examples, how children learn from the environment and from others around them.
- Define the four relational concepts: classification, seriation, spatial, and temporal.
- Identify ways in which children formulate concepts about their everyday world.

SETTING:

Type of situation (care center, nursery or preschool, kindergarten, family day care home, Head Start, private home, other) _____

Other information _____

Number of children present _____   Number of adults _____

Names and ages of children observed:

1. _____   Age _____

2. _____   Age _____

3. _____   Age _____

Time of day _____

TASK:

Respond to the following items after participating with and/or observing children at play.

Learning from One Another

1. Cite two situations that involved children teaching each other.

   a.

   b.

(Continued on next page)

Modeling

2. Describe how a child had opportunities to learn by watching someone else do the same thing.

Relational Concepts

3. On Chart 13-B list the activities and one child's behavior that indicated the child used materials involving *relational concepts*.

Chart 13-B
USING RELATIONAL CONCEPTS

Concept	Activities	Child's Behavior
Classification: (Grouping or matching objects that have like properties.)		
Example:	*Stringing large beads on string.*	*Child threaded three kinds of beads. Each had a hole. Some were round, some oblong, and some square. Child discarded same size objects that had no hole (small wooden marbles).*

(Continued on next page)

(Concept Formation—continued)

Chart 13-B
USING RELATIONAL CONCEPTS Continued

Concept	Activities	Child's Behavior
Seriation: (Placing objects in order according to graduated size.)		
Example:	*Random play with wooden cylinders that fit into holes in a long board.*	*Child placed each cylinder in the holes by trial and error until all were fitted into correct holes.*

(Continued on next page)

Chart 13-B
USING RELATIONAL CONCEPTS Continued

Concept	Activities	Child's Behavior
Spatial: (Manipulating objects in given spaces.)		
Example:	*Snack time, pouring juice.*	*Child poured small amount of juice from small pitcher into own glass without spilling.*

(Continued on next page)

Name _____ Date _____

(Concept Formation—continued)

Chart 13-B
USING RELATIONAL CONCEPTS Continued

Concept	Activities	Child's Behavior
Temporal: (Grasping the idea of the passage of time from one event to another.)		
Example:	*Child talking about experience at home.*	*Child said: "Tomorrow I went to the park with my sister." (Meaning yesterday.) The child knows the word <u>tomorrow</u> relates to time but does not have the idea of future tense.*

(Continued on next page)

Concept Formation

4. On Chart 13-C name five interest centers in which the child played (such as block area; home living center; and places for listening and reading, woodworking, science, art, etc.). Give examples of how the child experienced the same concept in each area.

Chart 13-C
FORMING CONCEPTS IN INTEREST AREAS

Interest Center	Concept	Describe the Child's Experience
Example: Woodworking	Back and forth.	Child used saw on board in back and forth motion. Adult said, "Karen, you are doing a good job of sawing back and forth, back and forth." Karen said, "See, back and forth."
Example: Home living center	Back and forth.	Child was rolling out playdough with rolling pin in back and forth motion. Adult said, "Oh, I see you are moving the rolling pin back and forth over the playdough. Rolling it back and forth will make a large flat piece, won't it?"

(Continued on next page)

(Concept Formation—continued)

Chart 13-C
FORMING CONCEPTS IN INTEREST AREAS Continued

Interest Center	Concept	Describe the Child's Experience

(Continued on next page)

EVALUATION:

1. *Imitation and modeling.*
Give three examples of how children learn from each other during play.

a.

b.

c.

List four examples of what children learn from watching or listening to others.

a.

b.

c.

d.

How can the environment help children learn?

2. *Relational concepts.*
Give examples during a child's play in which each of the four relational concepts are involved.
Classification:

Seriation:

Spatial:

Temporal:

3. *Concept formation.*
Give four examples of how children develop relational concepts through play.
a.

b.

c.

d.

LEVELS OF REPRESENTATION

(To accompany Chapter 13)

OBJECTIVES:
- Identify and describe four levels at which children represent reality.
- Discuss why the child must master one level of representation concerning a given object before moving to the next level.

SETTING:

Type of situation (care center, nursery or preschool, kindergarten, family day care home, Head Start, private home, other) _____

Other information _____

Number of children present _____ Number of adults _____

Name of child observed: _____ Age: _____

Time of day _____

TASK:

Record your experiences with one child in each of the following situations.

Representing Reality

1. On Chart 13-D check the levels at which the child was able to operate in a meaningful way. How well did the child appear to represent in his or her own mind the real object at each level? (You may have to list objects that were observed in place of those given on the chart.)

Chart 13-D
REPRESENTING THE REAL OBJECT

Levels of Representation	Objects	Meaning to the Child Was	
		Obvious	Not Obvious
Object Level: (Child plays with or interacts with the real object. Has opportunity to touch, see, taste, smell, hear as necessary to learn about object. Manipulates and uses object to learn about *purposes* and *properties* of object.) *Example:*	Book Apple Avocado Fish Telephone Car Other (identify) *Banana*	 x	

(Continued on next page)

Chart 13-D
REPRESENTING THE REAL OBJECT Continued

Levels of Representation	Objects	Meaning to the Child Was	
		Obvious	Not Obvious

Index Level:
 	
(Child uses one or more senses to get the idea of what the real object is without seeing or having the whole object present. A part of the real object may be present or simply a sound or smell from the real object.)
 	
Example:
	Book
	Apple
	Avocado
	Fish
	Telephone
	Car
	Other
	  (identify)
	Banana
	  (peeling)
		x
		
		Child saw and smelled the peeling.	

Symbol Level: (Picture or two-dimensional drawing or illustration of the real thing.) *Example:*	Book Apple Avocado Fish Telephone Car Other (identify) *Picture of a banana used during game time. The banana was peeled part way.*		x *Child called the picture a yellow flower like the one in her yard at home.*

(Continued on next page)

Chart 13-D

REPRESENTING THE REAL OBJECT Continued

Levels of Representation	Objects	Meaning to the Child Was	
		Obvious	Not Obvious
Sign Level: (The word that labels the real object.) *Example:*	Book Apple Avocado Fish Telephone Car Other (identify) *Banana*		x *The child made no reply when the word banana was seen in print.*

Levels of Representation

2. What activities did you see that indicated the level at which the child represented reality? How meaningful was each activity for the child in representing the real thing? Record your observations on Chart 13-E.

Chart 13-E

OBSERVING LEVELS OF REPRESENTATION

Level of Representation	Activity	Representation		
		Clear	Confusing	Meaningless
Object Level: (Activity with the real object.)				

(Continued on next page)

Chart 13-E
OBSERVING LEVELS OF REPRESENTATION Continued

Level of Representation	Activity	Representation		
		Clear	Confusing	Meaningless
Index Level: (An indication or reference to the real thing through one or more of the senses—touch, taste, sight, smell, sound.)				
Symbol Level: (A picture or two-dimensional representation of the real thing.)				
Sign Level: (The word which refers to the real thing.)				

EVALUATION:

1. Identify each *level of representation* and give an example of each.

2. *Levels of representation.*
Using examples of objects, describe how the child moves from one level to another in ability to represent the real thing.

3. *Continuing progress.*
How does knowledge of levels of representation help adults promote children's thinking skills in a meaningful way?

Name _____   Date _____

Course _____   Experience # _____

THINKING SKILLS

(*To accompany Chapter 13*)

OBJECTIVES:

- Identify basic tasks and skills which children achieve as part of their intellectual development.
- Explain the meaning of a step-by-step process of development over a period of time in the development of thinking skills.

SETTING:

Type of situation (care center, family day care home, nursery, preschool, Head Start, kindergarten,

private home, other) _____

Other information _____

Number of children present _____   Number of adults _____

Name of child _____   Age _____

Time of day _____

TASK:

Select one child and observe his or her level of thinking skills as reflected by the Chart 13-F checklist. You may have to make several observations to complete the list for each trial period.

Complete Trial I before beginning Trial II. Wait a few months after Trial I before making observations for Trial II. After several additional months, repeat the observations for Trial III. Compare the results of your observations for the three trial periods. Notice the progress made by the child in the given areas of development. "In some cases you may see changes in a matter of weeks."

Chart 13-F

CHECKLIST OF THINKING SKILLS

Date_____

Child's Name_____   Age_____

Trial I Date_____   Trial II Date_____   Trial III Date_____

Check the task or skill that you observe the child doing. Be sure the child can do the task or skill more than once so that you are not simply seeing a coincidence. When you wait a few months between trial periods, you are likely to see signs of the child's progress in developing concepts and ideas about the child's world.

Concept Area	Trial I	Trial II	Trial III
(The child may use words, actions, or both to convey the following concepts. Surrounding objects, the child alone, or other persons, may be used by the child to convey ideas. For example, you might observe that the child can match or use colors in a way that shows the child has the idea of *same* and *different* colors. She places all the yellow pegs together and discards those that are not yellow. She did not necessarily have to talk about the color yellow for you to know she has the concept of yellow in mind.)			

(Continued on next page)

Chart 13-F
CHECKLIST OF THINKING SKILLS Continued

Concept Area	Trial I	Trial II	Trial III
Shape concepts Circle			
Square			
Triangle			
Rectangle			
Rhombus (diamond shape)			
Hexagon			
Other shape (identify)			
Color concepts Red			
Yellow			
Blue			
Green			
Orange			
Purple			
Size concepts Large			
Not large			

(Continued on next page)

(Thinking Skills—continued)

Chart 13-F
CHECKLIST OF THINKING SKILLS Continued

Concept Area	Trial I	Trial II	Trial III
Big			
Not big			
Small			
Not small			
Little			
Not little			
Large, larger, largest			
Small, smaller, smallest			
Tall			
Short			
Long			
Thin			
Fat			
Concepts about how people feel Facial expressions: Happy			

(Continued on next page)

Chart 13-F
CHECKLIST OF THINKING SKILLS Continued

Concept Area	Trial I	Trial II	Trial III
Sad			
Angry			
Concepts of classifying (grouping and matching objects that are alike) Clothes with certain careers:			
Nurse			
Fireperson			
Policeperson			
Astronaut			
Objects during play: Size			
Shape			
Color			
Objects in room: Chairs and table			
Tapes and recorder			
Records and record player			
Puzzles on shelf			
Dishes in cupboard			

(Continued on next page)

Name _____ Date _____

(Thinking Skills—continued)

Chart 13-F

CHECKLIST OF THINKING SKILLS Continued

Concept Area	Trial I	Trial II	Trial III
Concepts of body parts Head			
Ears			
Nose			
Eyes			
Mouth			
Taste concepts Sweet			
Sour			
Bitter			
Salty			
Time concepts Morning			
Afternoon			
Night			
Day			

(Continued on next page)

Chart 13-F
CHECKLIST OF THINKING SKILLS Continued

Concept Area	Trial I	Trial II	Trial III
Age concepts Young			
Old			
Baby			
Child			
Youth			
Adult			
Position concepts Top—bottom			
High—low			
Far—near			
Under—over			
Above—below			
Front—back			
In—out			
Inside—outside			
At the side, beside, or next to			

(Continued on next page)

Name _____   Date _____

(Thinking Skills—continued)

Chart 13-F
CHECKLIST OF THINKING SKILLS Continued

Concept Area	Trial I	Trial II	Trial III
Between			
In the middle			
Auditory concepts Loud			
Soft			
High			
Low			
Texture concepts Hard			
Soft			
Smooth			
Rough			
Slick			
Fluffy			
Temperature concepts Hot			

(Continued on next page)

Chart 13-F
CHECKLIST OF THINKING SKILLS Continued

Concept Area	Trial I	Trial II	Trial III
Cold			
Warm			
Motion concepts Open—close (shut)			
Walk			
Run			
Skip			
Hop			
Tap			
Clap			
Wiggle			
Up—down			
In—out			
Stop—go			
Blink			
Wink			
Nod			

(Continued on next page)

Name _____ Date _____

(Thinking Skills—continued)

Chart 13-F
CHECKLIST OF THINKING SKILLS Continued

Concept Area	Trial I	Trial II	Trial III
Lift, carry			
Climb			
Jump			
Crawl			
Twist			
Dance			
Number concepts Counts objects up to five			
Counts objects up to 10			
Recognizes and identifies sets of One			
Two			
Three			
Concept of weight Heavy			
Light			

(Continued on next page)

Chart 13-F
CHECKLIST OF THINKING SKILLS Continued

Concept Area	Trial I	Trial II	Trial III
Gives address (street and number)			
Gives telephone number			
Demonstrates the meaning of position concepts by placement of objects Up—down			
In—out			
Over—under			
Knows seasons of the year and how they relate to events. *Example: School starts in the fall. Christmas comes in winter.* Winter			
Spring			
Summer			
Fall			
Draws human figures with Head			
Body			
Arms			
Legs			
Facial features			

(Continued on next page)

Name _____ Date _____

(Thinking Skills—continued)

Chart 13-F
CHECKLIST OF THINKING SKILLS Continued

Concept Area	Trial I	Trial II	Trial III
Hands			
Feet			
Recognizes "pairs" in relation to items, such as Shoes			
Socks			
Gloves			
Earrings			
Categorizes foods such as Vegetable			
Meat			
Bread			
Beverage			
Demonstrates concept of numbers from one to six by using objects or events			
Demonstrates concept of speed Fast			
Faster			

(Continued on next page)

Chart 13-F
CHECKLIST OF THINKING SKILLS Continued

Concept Area	Trial I	Trial II	Trial III
Slow			
Slower			
Demonstrates concept of numbers through ten			
Recognizes sets through six			
Is gaining awareness of cause and effect *Example: While it rains, there can be no outdoor play.*			
Demonstrates development of left to right eye movement			
Uses left to right eye movement			
Uses correct prepositions to denote place or position On			
In			
Under			
Behind			
Develops concept of "oneness" and "twoness" in relation to parts of the body (one nose, two ears)			
Demonstrates concept of "first" and "last" in relation to activities			

(Continued on next page)

Chart 13-F
CHECKLIST OF THINKING SKILLS Continued

Concept Area	Trial I	Trial II	Trial III
Groups animals according to living habits "Fish live in water."			
"Birds live in trees."			
Recalls happenings in sequence			
Is able to arrange picture puzzles in sequence of events			
Identifies coins (Penny, nickel, dime, quarter, dollar)			
Is developing a concept of the value of money			
Demonstrates knowledge that the printed sign represents the spoken word			
Extends matching concept to size, as big or little *Example: Placing blocks together or verbalizing and using contrasting sizes for specific purposes during block play.*			
Extends concept of counting to three; manipulates number concepts meaningfully in more than two by use of objects			
Acts out singly, or with others, simple stories that are familiar			

(Continued on next page)

EVALUATION:

1. Describe at least five basic tasks or skills which reflect a child's intellectual development.

    a.

    b.

    c.

    d.

    e.

2. Explain what is meant by a step-by-step process or sequence of development in the area of thinking skills.

Chapter 14
Language

Language, the basis of communication, uses symbols. These symbols make it possible to convey thoughts and feelings in a meaningful way. Language may be used in different forms such as writing, speaking, sign language, facial expression, body gesture, pantomime, and art. *Speech* is a form of language in which words or sounds are used to convey meanings. At first, the child's speech consists of sounds that are vague and difficult to understand. Gradually it progresses to clear and distinct words that carry specific messages. We call these messages controlled verbal communication.

Generally, by the age of three years, children are rapidly building their vocabularies. They continue to increase the number of words for the next few years.

Talking is one way of getting involved in learning activities. This helps children express ideas and thoughts. Besides this, words bring

Tony is developing skills for communicating as he learns to use the telephone.

Children like stories with body actions. Can you see how these gestures enhance the development of their language skills?

Amy likes to play with letters. She spells her name . . . among other things!

Darcey listens to a story she created herself. Later her dad wrote the story so she could listen to her own story being read by others. She learns that her words have meaning and value.

attention to the person who is talking. Communicating through speech provides one way of gaining some control over what is going to happen.

Elizabeth Hurlock, a child development authority, lists three essentials in learning to speak. These are basically the same as the requirements for learning motor skills. They include opportunities for practice, motivation to learn, and guidance in learning. In learning to speak, the child faces some major developmental tasks which are interrelated. These include: (1) comprehending, or understanding, the speech of others, (2) pronouncing words,

(3) building a vocabulary, and (4) combining words into sentences. The child must succeed in each task in the listed order to succeed in verbal language.

Language development includes social knowledge. As children interact with other humans and hear words being used, they learn what the words mean. They learn how to say and use the words. Children depend on other persons to provide models for their language development.

Children need many opportunities to practice their language skills. They do better in a relaxed situation. They generally talk about things that are of interest to them at the moment. Children usually begin to talk by using a combination of words and actions.

Name _____ Date _____

Course _____ Experience # _____

LANGUAGE DEVELOPMENT

(To accompany Chapter 14)

OBJECTIVES:

- Describe how children use concepts as they develop language skills.
- Explain how play helps a child develop language skills.
- List examples of children's language development as a result of listening to what others say (modeling).

SETTING:

Type of situation (care center, family day care home, nursery, preschool, Head Start, kindergarten,

private home, other)_____

Other information _____

Number of children present _____ Number of adults _____
Names and ages of children observed:

1. _____ Age _____

2. _____ Age _____

3. _____ Age _____

TASK:

Complete the following items as a result of participating and observing in a children's program or in a home.

Concepts

1. Record, verbatim (word for word), the child's statements which contain words that reflect concepts or ideas about objects. (*Big, little; soft hard; this is a tall man; this is a short, fat puppy,* etc.)

(Continued on next page)

2. Record five *location* or *prepositional* statements used by children. (*Under, over, behind, under-neath, beside, inside, next to, on top of,* etc.) Give the child's sentences verbatim.

a.

b.

c.

d.

e.

Language Concepts

3. Record four statements using *polar* (opposite) *concepts.* (*Wide, narrow; big, little; short, tall; hot, cold,* etc.)

a.

b.

c.

d.

Language Development

4. Record five statements which indicated children sometimes use words incorrectly even though they think they are accurate.

a.

b.

(Language Development—continued)

    c.

    d.

    e.

Modeling

5. Record five statements or words which indicated that children learn by listening to others.
    a.

    b.

    c.

    d.

    e.

6. List ways adults *modeled* language for children. What did they purposely say in order to provide an example for the children?

(Continued on next page)

Labels

7. List words that children used to label objects. (*"This* red *spool goes here." "I have a* circle *hanging on my necklace."*)

EVALUATION:
Concepts

1. Give examples of concepts used by children as they develop language skills.

Language Skills

2. List three ways that children can develop language skills during play.
   a.

   b.

   c.

Modeling

3. Why is it important for adults to talk with children during their daily activities?

COMMUNICATION SKILLS

(To accompany Chapter 14)

OBJECTIVES:

- Identify and record specific examples of a child's need to communicate effectively.
- Explain how everyday play experiences help children learn to communicate.

SETTING:

Type of situation (care center, nursery, preschool, Head Start, family day care home, kindergarten, private home, other) _____

Other information _____

Number of children present _____   Number of adults _____

Names and ages of children observed:

1. _____   Age _____

2. _____   Age _____

3. _____   Age _____

Time of day _____

TASK:

As you interact with children or observe them, record examples and evidence of how they develop communication skills.

Learning To Communicate

1. What specific help was provided by the teacher or parent for the children to develop skills for communicating?

2. How did adults attempt to meet the needs of children for improving their communication skills?

(Continued on next page)

3. What activities were used for this purpose?

Adult-Child Communications

4. How did adults respond to children during moments of stress? Describe at least one situation.

5. Give a detailed description of how a child communicated specific needs (food, play, personal needs, etc.) to an adult when the child's language was not adequately developed.

6. Record three instances in which a child needed to communicate with another child or adult but did not have the vocabulary or language skills needed. Describe what the child did to get his or her message understood. How successful was the child?

   a.

(Communication Skills—continued)

  b.

  c.

EVALUATION:

 1. List five examples that reflect a child's need to communicate effectively.
  a.

  b.

  c.

  d.

  e.

(Continued on next page)

2. Give examples of how communication skills develop through the following:
   a. Everyday play experiences.

   b. Motivation from within the child.

   c. Guidance and encouragement from adults.

Name _____   Date _____

Course _____   Experience # _____

LANGUAGE SKILLS

(To accompany Chapter 14)

OBJECTIVES:

- Describe ways by which children develop language skills.
- Explain the necessity of opportunities, motivation, and guidance to help children develop language skills.

SETTING:

Type of situation (care center, nursery, preschool, Head Start, family day care home, kindergarten, private home, other) _____

Other information _____

Number of children present _____   Number of adults _____

Names and ages of children observed:

1. _____   Age _____

2. _____   Age _____

3. _____   Age _____

Time of day _____

TASK:

Observe and record evidence of how children develop language skills in a home setting or in a children's center.

Learning Language

1. List opportunities which enabled the child to practice while learning to speak.

(Continued on next page)

Motivation

2. List specific situations that encouraged the child to want to learn language.

Speech and Language

3. List specific actions of the adults that helped promote the child's speech and language development.

Developmental Tasks

4. Observe a child in a home or in a center. (For example, in a home—parent-child activities such as games, puzzles, storytelling. In a center—teacher-children activities such as dramatic play, music, meal or snack time, table games.) On Chart 14-A record evidence that the child was achieving developmental tasks in speech and language. Where possible, record verbatim (word for word) what the child said and what the adult said.

Chart 14-A
OBSERVING DEVELOPMENTAL ACHIEVEMENT

Developmental Task	Evidence—What Happened
Understanding or comprehending the speech of others.	

(Continued on next page)

Name _____ Date _____

(Language Skills—continued)

Chart 14-A
OBSERVING DEVELOPMENTAL ACHIEVEMENT Continued

Developmental Task	Evidence—What Happened
Pronouncing words.	
Building a vocabulary (learning new words).	
Combining words into sentences.	

EVALUATION:

1. How can adults and older children help young children develop their language skills?

2. Why is it necessary for a child to feel comfortable and relaxed when learning to talk?

Chapter 15
Social Skills

Children learn to be social by being with others. This begins early in life. The infant's first social experiences start with the mother at birth. Social contacts soon include other family members. Gradually the child is able to extend social contacts beyond the family.

People are social creatures and want to be accepted by those around them. Children are eager to please others. They soon learn what types of behavior receive attention and response. These behaviors are often repeated.

Parents influence their children in learning social skills. For example, a baby learns what to expect from parents by their day to day behavior. How children get along with others and how they cope with everyday situations depends greatly on their experiences. It depends on the early interactions they have with parents and other children.

Socialization is a process by which children learn to fit in and become an accepted member of society. The family is the first social experience for the child. Child care centers often play a significant part in the socialization process.

Darcey gets a demonstration of paring the pear. As she describes some of its properties she becomes interested in this food.

Now for the slicing—then she can pass the slices to the other children.

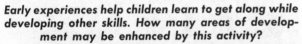

Early experiences help children learn to get along while developing other skills. How many areas of development may be enhanced by this activity?

Here's helpful Amy again. She and Billie Jo develop social skills as they cooperate to work the same puzzle. Can you see how children learn from each other?

This is true especially for children whose parents both work outside the home. One-parent families rely heavily on child care centers to provide social experiences for their children.

Recent research indicates that children as young as one year of age begin playing together. They appear to form early friendships this way. In addition to play and contacts with others, there are other social skills. Examples include such tasks as feeding oneself, dressing, toileting, and grooming. These are called social because they help one be accepted by others. Children learn many of these social skills from other family members.

In order to live a meaningful life, children must learn to use symbols and signs that represent parts of the real world. These symbols and signs are man-made. We refer to knowledge about these as social knowledge because they are created and passed on by society. For example, people label objects to identify them. Take the example of a simple shape—a *blue triangle.* A child develops concepts and ideas by playing with this object. Even so, the knowledge about verbal labels of color and shape will not become a part of the child's mental system until someone talks about these properties with the child. For instance, Amy heard her father refer to the color as blue and to the shape as a triangle. She learned these labels and others through play. This is social knowledge. When Amy learns to read, she will be able to gain additional social knowledge. The letters and their arrangements into sentences are also man-made. They have social significance. Various cultures and societies have their own systems and symbols that are used to create a common language. The language becomes a major social tool for communicating in a given society.

Certain behaviors are acceptable in a social group. For example, patterns of eating vary from one culture to another. They even vary between social groups of one given culture.

Attitudes and values reflect a person's philosophy about life. These attitudes and values are formed within a social setting. Children often take on the attitudes and values of their parents. They are also influenced by persons closest to them during the early years of life. Attitudes may change and values may be rejected. This is often a result of learning. Nevertheless, some family influences are believed to prevail throughout a person's life.

Name _____   Date _____

Course _____   Experience # _____

SOCIALIZATION

(To accompany Chapter 15)

OBJECTIVES:

- Describe clues to the socialization of children—how they learn to get along with others.
- Identify situations where children are attempting to gain approval from adults.
- Explain how adults influence children's development of everyday living skills such as eating habits, dressing themselves, toileting, sharing toys, and respecting other persons and property.

SETTING:

Type of situation (care center, family day care home, nursery or preschool, kindergarten, private

home, Head Start, other) _____

Other information _____

Number of children present _____   Number of adults _____
Names and ages of children observed:

1. _____   Age _____

2. _____   Age _____

3. _____   Age _____

Time of day _____

TASK:

Record attempts by adults to intervene in the child's activity. Observe how the child responds to the adults. Notice how children learn from others about everyday tasks and getting along together.

Social Behavior

1. Write a brief description of the behavior of a child between ages two and three who is learning to share and get along with others.

(Continued on next page)

Write a brief description of the same type of behavior of a child between ages four and five.

2. What did the adult do in any attempts to change a child's behavior?

3. How effective was the method?

Social Skills

4. List behavior or skills that children appeared to be learning from each other. *Example:* How to put toys away after use.

5. Observe a child long enough to see what happens with the toileting process.

Did the child say anything to an adult about the need to toilet? Yes _____ No _____
What was said? By child:

By adult:

Name _____ Date _____

(Socialization—continued)

Did the child manage own clothing in the process? Yes _____ No _____ Describe what occurred.

Did the child flush the toilet? Yes _____ No _____

Did the child wash hands adequately? Yes _____ No _____ Describe what happened.

Did the adult give the child any encouragement during the toileting process or make any comments

when the task was complete? Yes _____ No _____
Record comments made by adult and child:

(Continued on next page)

6. Observe two children dressing or undressing themselves. Describe what each child did. If either child received help from an adult, explain what happened and what was said by both child and adult.

EVALUATION:

Social Behavior

1. Describe examples of clues that children give which show they are developing the ability to get along with others.

2. List ways that children attempt to gain approval from adults.

(Socialization—continued)

3. How can adults help children develop acceptable behavior?

Daily Living Skills

4. Identify specific ways children learn daily living skills.

Name _____ Date _____

Course _____ Experience # _____

SOCIAL COMPETENCIES: DAILY LIVING SKILLS

(To accompany Chapter 15)

OBJECTIVES:
- Identify clues that indicate the level of a child's daily living skills (socialization).
- Describe how children learn and develop skills that help them meet daily tasks and expectations.
- Explain how children's motor coordination helps them develop social skills.
- Give examples of how children learn through their senses.

SETTING:

Type of situation (care center, family day care home, nursery, preschool, kindergarten, private

home, Head Start, other) _____

Other information _____

Number of children present _____ Number of adults _____

Name of child observed _____ Age (months) _____

Type of food service: Mealtime _____ Snack time _____

Food served: _____

Room and table arrangements: _____

_____

Time of day _____

TASK:

On Chart 15-A record observations of one child during meal or snack time. You may have to observe for several days to get all the information needed. (Notice the example.)

Chart 15-A
EATING BEHAVIOR

	Always	Some-times	Never	Evidences
Motor Skills *Example:* *Held cup or glass with one hand.*		√		*Used both hands sometimes.*
Held cup or glass with both hands.				
Controlled spoon, fork, or knife with hands and fingers.				
Chewed food adequately.				
Poured milk or other beverage.				
Cut with a knife.				

(Continued on next page)

Chart 15-A
EATING BEHAVIOR Continued

	Always	Some-times	Never	Evidences
Used a napkin.				
Sensory Experiences Handled food while eating.				
Smelled or tasted food before eating it.				
Placed food in mouth with fingers.				
Eating Habits Messy.				
Neat.				
Dawdled.				
Eating Patterns Carefully separated foods on plate before eating.				
Ate all of one food, then another until completing meal.				
Ate some of each food in an alternating pattern.				
Wanted to know about any food that looked unfamiliar.				
Ate dessert before completing other foods.				
Drank beverage completely before eating food.				
Drank beverage along with meal.				
Drank beverage after completing meal.				
Communication Skills Talked with others during meal or snack time.				
Talked with children next to him or her.				
Talked with child across the table or room.				
Talked with adults nearby.				
Talked with adults across the room.				
Had pleasant conversation.				
Spent more time interacting with others than eating.				
Managed to eat and interact at the same time.				

(Continued on next page)

Name _____ Date _____

(Social Competencies: Daily Living Skills—continued)

Chart 15-A
EATING BEHAVIOR Continued

	Always	Some-times	Never	Evidences
Ate without talking or interacting.				
Food Preferences Had obvious likes and dislikes.				
Talked about foods he or she liked.				
Actions without words reflected food preferences.				
Adult Intervention Did an adult encourage the child to develop manipulative skills (by allowing the child to do things such as pour, spread, cut, peel, and feed self)?				
Was the child encouraged to use the senses to explore the way food feels, tastes, and smells?				
Did the child receive some individual attention?				
Was the child encouraged to try new foods?				
Was the child encouraged to eat all of the food and complete the meal or snack?				
Was dawdling or other non-eating activity ignored?				
Completion of Meal or Snack and Leaving the Table Did the child comment about the food?				
Did the child continue to interact with others who were still eating?				
Did the child help clear the table?				
Scraped his or her plate.				
Stacked dishes and flatware.				
Carried eating utensils to designated place.				
Wiped table with sponge or cloth.				
Other helping tasks (identify).				
Child was boisterous or noisy.				

(Continued on next page)

Chart 15-A

EATING BEHAVIOR Continued

	Always	Some-times	Never	Evidences
Child was unobtrusive or hardly noticed in exit from table.				
Activities following Meal Washed face and hands.				
Went to toilet.				
Became involved in quiet activity.				
Ran about.				
Other (explain).				

EVALUATION:

1. Cite examples that help identify the child's level of skill in eating.

2. What are some specific activities that provide opportunities for children to develop daily living skills?

(Social Competencies: Daily Living Skills—continued)

3. How does the child combine motor coordination and the use of the senses in developing social skills?

Chapter 16
Emotional Development

Emotion is a mental state that brings about the expression of how one feels. Emotions range from feelings of great pleasure to feelings of great pain. Emotions may result in sudden outbursts of how a person feels at the moment. On the other hand, subtle and hardly noticed feelings may develop over a long period of time. Emotions that result from pleasant experiences may be expressed as love, affection, joy, happiness, and contentment. Unpleasant experiences may result in emotional expressions of anger, fear, hatred, pain, and disappointment.

Feelings are believed to begin when the baby associates comfort and warmth with a feeling of happiness and contentment. The baby may also associate discomfort with fear, anger, or frustration. Infants soon learn a variety of ways to express their feelings. Examples range from crying to laughing. You see this as you watch babies. A colorful jingling object may bring laughter and gurgling. On the other hand, wet diapers or hunger usually cause the baby to cry or fuss. Emotions and social abilities are so closely related they are often referred to as social-emotional development.

Children need to experience the feelings of others as they grow and develop. A child's self-concept is influenced by the way others treat the child. Love and affection not only promote healthy development of the child's self-concept, but the child learns these responses from others.

Negative feelings are generally expressed through such responses as anger, crying, hostility, and bitterness. Children who receive lots of negative response over a long period of time may develop negative feelings about themselves.

Children will, of course, experience both positive and negative responses. They usually

Children enjoy giving love as well as receiving it.

Sometimes children use puppets to help them express their feelings. Mrs. Adams and Jeremy enjoy a dialogue with the help of Willie-the-Worm. Children also feel secure when they receive gentle and kind responses from others.

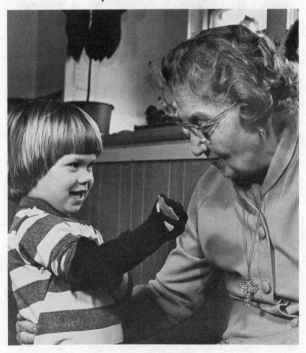

Children need to feel free to express a variety of feelings. Even stumbling in the grass can be frustrating at times.

A little comfort and special attention help children cope with stressful moments.

express these feelings openly. Some are more obvious than others. Young children often show their excitement and joy by a combination of words, facial expressions, and body movements. For instance: Randy shrieked with joy. His eyes and mouth opened wide and he jumped up and down. He succeeded in blowing a soap bubble!

Children may show negative feelings by acting out, or misbehaving. For instance: Ellen jerked the doll away from Todd. She began to beat it harshly.

You can help children learn to express themselves appropriately. They learn from others who serve as models. When they see adults express anger and hostility in destructive ways, they think it is all right to do the same. They also learn to express such feelings as love and affection through examples they see in the behavior of others.

As you interact with children you will see the many ways they express their feelings. You will need to provide ways for children to express their feelings in everyday experiences. Let children know you understand they have feelings. Children need to feel free to express both positive and negative feelings.

Name _____ Date _____

Course _____ Experience # _____

EMOTIONS

(To accompany Chapter 16)

OBJECTIVES:

- Define emotions.
- Discuss the differences between positive and negative emotions.
- Explain why it is important for children to express their feelings during play.
- Explain how adults influence children's emotional development.

SETTING:

Type of situation (care center, family day care home, nursery, preschool, kindergarten, Head Start,

private home, other) _____

Other information _____

Number of children present _____ Number of adults _____

Names and ages of children observed:

1. _____ Age _____

2. _____ Age _____

3. _____ Age _____

Time of day _____

TASK:

Respond to the following items.

Expressing Feelings

1. Describe two situations in which children showed emotions. Report what happened to bring about the emotional response. What did the child say and do in each case?

    a.

(Continued on next page)

b.

2. Describe a situation in which a child expressed positive feelings. Explain how the child responded. What did the child say and do in the given situation? What did the adult say and do?

Describing Emotions

3. As you watched children playing with one another, what adjectives first came to your mind that described a child's emotional state? (*Joyful, angry, tense,* etc.) On Chart 16-A list the positive words and the negative words that describe what you saw.

Chart 16-A
EMOTIONAL STATES

Positive	Negative

Name _____ Date _____

(Emotions—continued)

4. Observe one particular child. How did the child react to frustration or disappointment?

5. How did the same child react to satisfaction and pleasure?

Behavior

6. As a result of your involvement with children, or your observations of them, describe how they behaved when experiencing the following:

Aggression:

Withdrawal:

Joy:

Frustration:

Dependence on others:

Happiness:

(Continued on next page)

Satisfaction:

Fear:

Fantasy:

Anxiety:

Adult-Child Relations

7. Describe what you saw adults do in the following situations:
   a. When a child was crying—
      Why was the child crying?

      What did the adult do?

      How did the child respond?

   b. When a child became angry—
      Why was the child angry?

(Emotions—continued)

What did the adult do?

How did the child respond?

c. When a child hit another or tried to take a toy away—
Why did the child hit another?

What did the adult do?

How did the child respond?

d. When a child accomplished a task with success—
What task did the child accomplish?

(Continued on next page)

What did the adult do?

How did the child respond?

Emotional Response

8. Describe a child's reaction to any of the following situations that took place while you were participating or observing.
   a. One child watching another child crying.

   b. One child watching another child receiving help from an adult in a mishap (such as spilled milk or a broken toy).

   c. One child watching other children accidentally getting hurt (such as bumping heads or falling).

EVALUATION:

1. Define emotions.

(Emotions—continued)

2. Give two examples of positive emotions and two examples of negative emotions. Cite examples of how these emotions are expressed during play.

3. Discuss the importance of expressing positive and negative emotions.

4. Explain how adults can help or hinder children in their emotional development.

Chapter 17
Guiding Children's Behavior

Behavior refers to what the child is doing. Actions and reactions that result from a combination of thoughts and feelings make up behavior. Behavior may be of three types:

• *Positive behavior*—actions and reactions that are appropriate in a given *time, place,* and *situation.* Positive behavior may also be called acceptable or good behavior.

• *Negative behavior*—actions and reactions that are not appropriate in *time, place,* or *situation.* This type of behavior may also be called unacceptable or bad.

• *Exceptional behavior*—actions and reactions that are not usually acceptable but are allowed for special reasons. For example, a child may pour objects out of a container onto the floor. She may be exploring something new

in her environment. Her behavior is tolerated because her parents know she is learning by exploring. Gradually, they will help her learn what objects she can play with freely and which ones require special care.

You can do much to help children develop self-discipline. This means they can direct much of their own behavior. Children learn from watching and imitating the behavior of others. This makes it important to serve as a good model. The way one talks and behaves toward children influences how the children respond. It also sets an example. Children generally respond in a positive way to persons who treat them with respect and understanding.

Even when children are too young to talk, they develop feelings about others. This often

When children have a great variety of appropriate experiences in which they can explore through their senses, they are less likely to have behavior problems.

Dennis gets a positive response from Amy as she helps him with his jacket. Don't you think Amy has had some good models?

Carlton develops a sense of responsibility as he shares in the care of plants.

George exercises patience and gives support as children are encouraged to do things for themselves.

depends on how they are treated and cared for each day.

Consistency is needed as you interact with children. They need to know what they can expect day after day. Responding to children in about the same way under similar circumstances helps them feel comfortable with your behavior. They know about what to expect. For example, Leo learned quickly that he must replace the saws and hammers after using them at the carpentry table. He learned what was expected because his teacher insisted that this be done each day. He had to be encouraged at first so he would develop a habit of putting things away. The point is that he was not allowed to leave the tools on the table or floor. He put them away before going on to other activities. He learned that he was expected to replace the tools.

Children generally respond best to positive encouragement from adults. When you see children behave in appropriate ways, comment about their behavior. This reinforces their desire to behave in the same manner again.

As you are around children, become aware of their thoughts, attitudes, and feelings about others and about themselves. This will help you understand why they behave the way they do. Children give clues about their behavior. You can develop the ability to follow these clues and gain insight into each child's situation.

Above all, children must be treated with respect and dignity. This must be done regardless of how difficult a situation may seem to be. It is better to take no action than to take disrespectful action toward a child. You can be firm and kind without being destructive. Children may need lots of support and encouragement to channel their energies into positive actions. Children need help to develop the ability to direct their own behavior in a responsible way. Children need *freedom of expression.* They need *alternatives to choose from.* They need *direction.* Children need help from adults in setting *limits.* Keep these concerns in mind as you interact with children.

GUIDING BEHAVIOR

(To accompany Chapter 17)

OBJECTIVES:

- Define positive and negative behavior.
- Discuss the value of being consistent with children in setting limits.
- Explain the value of helping children develop the ability to direct their own behavior in a responsible way.

SETTING:

Type of situation (care center, nursery, preschool, Head Start, family day care home, kindergarten,

private home, other)_____

Other information _____

Number of children present _____   Number of adults _____

Names and ages of children observed:

1. _____   Age _____

2. _____   Age _____

3. _____   Age _____

Time of day _____

TASK:

Respond to the following items as you observe children's behavior while watching them and/or while participating in activities with them.

Expressing Feelings

1. Identify one child and record, word for word, what the child said during the following situations that reflect the child's feelings.

    a. Cooperative play with one or more children. (Describe the setting and include as much conversation as possible.)

(Continued on next page)

b. Story time.

c. Art or creative activities.

d. When the child arrived at the center and the parent departed, or in a home when the parent departed.

(Guiding Behavior—continued)

    e. Sharing toys.

    f. Dramatic play in which the child pretended to be someone else such as "mother" or "father" or "baby."

  2. Observe the same child in several situations. Notice the child's behavior, including the expression of feelings. How did the child's feelings match the child's behavior? Rate the child in each situation.

    a. Cooperative play with one or more children.
    Behavior:

(Continued on next page)

What feelings did the child express?

_____ Somewhat happy	_____ Very happy
_____ Somewhat troubled	_____ Content
_____ Unhappy	_____ Sad
_____ Hostile	_____ Angry
	_____ No obvious feelings

b. Story time.
   Behavior:

What feelings did the child express?

_____ Somewhat happy	_____ Very happy
_____ Somewhat troubled	_____ Content
_____ Unhappy	_____ Sad
_____ Hostile	_____ Angry
	_____ No obvious feelings

c. Art or creative activities.
   Behavior:

What feelings did the child express?

_____ Somewhat happy	_____ Very happy
_____ Somewhat troubled	_____ Content
_____ Unhappy	_____ Sad
_____ Hostile	_____ Angry
	_____ No obvious feelings

3. Dealing with conflict.
   Identify a child and describe what the child said and/or what the child did during a conflict:

(Guiding Behavior—continued)

Adult Examples

4. On Chart 17-A list four or five ways that adults set examples for children to develop positive or negative behavior patterns. (Notice the examples.)

Chart 17-A
EXAMPLES SET BY ADULTS

Situation	Positive or Negative	What the Adult Does and Says
Example: Mealtime	Negative	Adult pours milk for three-year-old Randy. Adult says: "Randy, let me pour your milk so you won't spill it. It's too much work to clean up after you kids."
Example: Mealtime	Positive	Adult places small pitcher and small glass near three-year-old Randy's plate. Adult says: "Randy, I will pour some milk into your pitcher, and you may pour your own milk." (Child spills a little on table.) Adult: "Oh, a little accident. Here is a sponge. You may wipe up the spill."
a.		
b.		

(Continued on next page)

Chart 17-A
EXAMPLES SET BY ADULTS Continued

Situation	Positive or Negative	What the Adult Does and Says
c.		
d.		
e.		

Being Kind and Consistent

5. Record what adults said to children that show consistent or inconsistent patterns of discipline. (You may use other situations in place of the following.)

IN A HOME SETTING

a. While a child was getting dressed.

b. When a child wanted to play with something that was not to be used as a toy (such as mother's knitting equipment).

IN A CHILDREN'S CENTER

c. When a child was not cooperating in a group with other children.

d. During naptime when the child did not want to lie down.

(Continued on next page)

Learning Behavior from Other Children

6. On Chart 17-B cite examples of how children learned positive or negative behavior from others.

Chart 17-B
LEARNING FROM OTHER CHILDREN

Example	Positive	Negative	What Happened? Who Said What?
a.			
b.			
c.			
d.			

(Continued on next page)

(Guiding Behavior—continued)

Chart 17-B
LEARNING FROM OTHER CHILDREN Continued

Example	Positive	Negative	What Happened? Who Said What?
e.			
f.			
g.			
h.			

Chapter 18
Creativity in Children

Play is one process which brings about creativity. Children reflect their creativity through play. Creativity, here, refers to the child's novel, or new, ideas and feelings. These may be expressed in facial expressions or body movements. They may be reflected by words or actions. A combination of these is also common. Children learn to solve problems by using creative thinking.

The following indicators or clues will help you observe creativity in children.

• The ability to change a play situation without disrupting the activities or upsetting the other children. For example, a creative child is one who can move in and out of groups. This child will enjoy the interaction with others and the activity as well. A creative child can use a toy in several different ways.

• The expression of exciting and joyful thoughts and feelings. Children show what they are thinking and how they are feeling through facial gestures and body motions. They also do this with words or sounds.

• The ability to laugh about oneself and show the lighter side of a situation. For example, the child who gently teases playmates creates a fun-filled atmosphere.

• The expression of spontaneous (all-of-a-sudden) thoughts and feelings through a variety of activities. Examples include use of play-dough, carpentry materials, puppets, painting, dance and body movements, dramatic play, and problem-solving activities.

Children reflect their creativity as they use toys such as dolls in many different ways. They are able to modify, or change the toy to make it more useful and more fun. They do this as they

Ramoan is able to use materials and equipment in a variety of ways.

Art activities allow children to try out their ideas and express their feelings.

Little Alistair enjoys the world of make-believe. He and Ramoan use puppets to explore the roles of the worm and the dragon.

play either alone or with other children. As they hear stories, children may create their own versions. They often do this by putting characters and situations together in new ways. Children also show their creativity by the use of fantasy and absurdity. They enjoy pretending and playing imaginary roles.

Play provides opportunities for children to respond in their own unique ways to objects and people. Through play, children can try their new ideas.

Scribbling with finger paints made of soap flakes and water allows Nathan to explore through his senses.

Name _____ Date _____

Course _____ Experience # _____

CREATIVITY

(To accompany Chapter 18)

OBJECTIVES:

- Discuss the meaning of creative activities.
- Describe ways that children express creativity through ideas and thoughts.
- Cite examples of ways children express feelings through play and play materials.

SETTING:

Type of situation (care center, family day care home, nursery, preschool, kindergarten, Head Start,

private home, other) _____

Other information _____

Number of children present _____ Number of adults _____

Names and ages of children observed:

1. _____ Age _____

2. _____ Age _____

3. _____ Age _____

Time of day _____

TASK:

Respond to the items below as you participate with children or observe them in the following types of activities:

finger painting   working with wood
clay or playdough   cutting and pasting
easel painting   water play
block play   food experiences (preparing food, cooking, etc.)
sand play   dramatic play

Expression of Feelings

1. What *feelings, impressions,* and *ideas* did you see expressed by a child? Give an example of each.

Feelings:

Impressions and ideas:

(Continued on next page)

Creative Movements

2. What physical or body-type activities did you see a child involved in that indicated the child's desire to express ideas or thoughts?

Interest Span

3. How long did one child remain interested in the same activity?

Describe the activity and what the child did.

Freedom to Explore

4. List specific opportunities children had to freely explore the materials used in activities with:
Playdough or clay:

Paints and paper:

Pasting and cutting:

Woodworking:

Sand or water play:

226

Creativity

5. List types of activities which made it possible for children to put ideas together in new ways.

6. Describe examples of how children were able to use materials and thoughts to create new situations that had meaning for them.

EXAMPLE: John wanted to play with a truck that Jane was using. She said she wanted to play with it. John went to the block area and took one long block and one short block off the shelf. He then asked for the clear tape. He managed to tape the small block to the large one and used the object as a truck. He told Jane, "See my truck."

7. Explain how a child used ideas and materials to solve a problem.

EXAMPLE: Jeremy was using playdough at the table with several children. Two children were using rolling pins with the playdough. Without saying anything, Jeremy went to the block area and picked up a wooden cylinder about six inches long and went back to the playdough with "his rolling pin."

(Continued on next page)

EVALUATION:

1. Did you consider any of the children's activities more of an opportunity for "freedom of expression" than actual creativity? Yes _____ No _____ Discuss the difference and give an example of each.

2. Explain what it means for a child to be creative in solving a problem.

3. Describe ways that children express feelings through play and play materials.

Chapter 19
Program Administration and Management

Management of a children's center begins with identifying goals for the children. The children's activities, physical facilities, room arrangement, daily routines and schedule, equipment, and materials can be managed to accomplish certain goals. Examples of these goals include social-emotional development, language skills, motor coordination, thinking skills, and living skills. Certain considerations are necessary for operating a program. Examples include advanced planning by the staff, goals and objectives, the program design, and a team approach. These are all centered around working with the children.

The indoor and outdoor spaces of a children's center or a home provide the setting for the children's daily activities. Here they live, learn, play, work, rest, and eat. This is where they interact with each other and with adults. The following examples of interest areas help children choose daily activities that are meaningful to them.

- *Block and Large Toy Area*—Enough space for freedom to move about out of traffic lanes. The area is equipped with large blocks for building constructions and large toys.
- *Dramatic Play/Homemaking Center*—Preferably a corner arrangement with child-size sink, refrigerator, stove, table and chairs, dishes, dolls, doll bed, dress-up clothes, and a full-length mirror. This area may be changed periodically to provide such settings as a store, post office, barber and beauty shops, and bakery.
- *Store/Shopping Center*—Area might include a cash register, check-out counter, shelves with simulated groceries, play money, and grocery sacks.
- *Library/Reading Center*—Carpet or rug on the floor, quiet, and comfortable setting with "easy" chairs or cushions, bookshelves clearly display books at children's eye level.
- *Art and Creative Media*—Easy-to-clean floors, easel, paper and painting supplies, clay, playdough, scissors, paste, table, and display area.

- *Table Area*—Games and manipulative activities such as puzzles, lottos, peg boards, sewing cards, beads, lacing frames, and nuts and bolts.
- *Music and Creative Movements*—Record player or tape recorder, piano, and/or autoharp, various rhythm instruments; room for free and easy body movements.
- *Science Center*—Pets, plants, equipment for science experiments such as weights and measures, cooking utensils, and aquariums and terrariums.
- *Carpentry*—Workbench with tools for cutting and building. Equipment includes such items as hammers, nails, drills, sandpaper, and wood. Easy-to-clean floor covering.
- *Water and Sand Play*—Portable water/sand table for use indoors as well as outdoors.

A *daily schedule* is needed. Planning in advance for each day's activities is important. It prepares the environment for children's activities. These lead toward achieving the goals. Flexibility is possible by having a plan. This is like a map for guiding the way. The plan can be altered to meet the needs of individual children. Children need activities that allow them to pursue interests and motivations at their own developmental levels. Children like to have a general routine. This helps them learn about limitations and guidelines. A routine helps them participate in daily activities with a sense of security.

Working with children in *small groups* of five or six in each is helpful. This allows adults to give more individual attention and assistance to the children. In small groups, each child has many opportunities to participate and contribute. This enhances language development, self-concept, sensory acuity, and concept formation. Each child develops social skills by communicating and interacting with others. Children are capable of working together in small groups with little supervision. Of course, it is good to have an adult near and available for help when needed.

John returns the symbol he wore while in the book nook. Notice the matching necklaces hanging below each symbol which represent the activity areas. (Each activity area has a large matching symbol hanging from the ceiling.)

"Now, I'm ready." John assumes the responsibility for his choice by wearing the necklace until he is ready to go to another area. This management technique also provides opportunities for developing concepts about shapes, color, spacial arrangements of the room, independence, and social skills.

John decides to work in the art area. This calls for wearing a necklace with a yellow circle.

An organized arrangement of equipment and materials enhances the setting for children's play. Carlton enjoys the simple task of returning these play objects to the shelves.

Children enjoy exploring and learning in a comfortable and natural way. Some children will wait to be told or shown what to do. They need concerned adults who encourage them. Children also need time to do things independently. This means time to be alone, without the help or interference from others. The best planning provides both individualized and group time for children.

A *team approach* gives flexibility and strength to a children's program. Children are not concerned about which adult has the most training or highest degree. Each child responds to those adults who interact in a comfortable and effective way. The team makes it possible to plan together. Each team member knows the total scope of the program and what is to take place. Each adult usually assumes a role in the activities which uses that adult's special talents. Still all the staff must be acquainted with the program and the children. Each should be able to float or move from one group to another as necessary. Each adult must be able to respond to a variety of children's needs.

The *equipment* and *supplies* are selected and used to achieve goals for the children. Activities should lead to the achievement of each child's full potential. Managing a program includes the use and upkeep of equipment as well as selection. All items must be safe and in good working condition.

A team approach provides for sharing ideas among teachers, parents, and volunteers.

Children enjoy colorful surroundings in which incidental learning occurs.

Simply decorated window shades provide concept formation possibilities while serving as an attractive background for the plants and aquarium.

Name _____   Date _____

Course _____   Experience # _____

ADMINISTRATION: OPERATING A CHILDREN'S CENTER

(To accompany Chapter 19)

OBJECTIVES:

- Define administration.
- List five qualifications for an administrator.
- Identify and describe the major tasks involved in operating a children's center.

SETTING:

Type of situation (care center, family day care home, nursery, preschool, kindergarten, Head Start, other)_____

Other information _____

Number of children present _____   Number of adults _____

Time of day _____

TASK:

As you participate or observe a children's program, record activities of the administrator. Discuss the operation of the center with the administrator. Record your findings about how the center operated.

Administrative Tasks

1. What activities did you observe which were related to administration or operating the center? By the director:

(Continued on next page)

By the lead teacher or coordinator:

By the teachers:

By the others (name each position):

2. Did the children appear to respond the same way to the various adults on the center staff? Did the children look to one person as most important? Or did children appear to respond to all adults in about the same way? Explain by giving examples.

Operating a Center

3. How did the adults carry out daily tasks that kept the center operating? Check appropriate response.

Each person worked alone on certain tasks. _____

The teachers worked as a team. _____

The children could not tell who was the lead teacher or who was the assistant. _____

The director told each person what to do. _____

Everyone seemed to know what to do. _____

The adults working with the children asked the lead teacher what to do. _____

4. Interview the administrator and fill out the following questionnaire.
   a. Who does the following tasks?

   Hire personnel _____

   Write the job descriptions _____

   Develop the overall plan for the program _____

   Implement the program _____

   Evaluate the program _____

   Set up the program _____

   Incorporate parents _____

(Continued on next page)

Recruit the children   _____

Set up the children's center, including room arrangements, equip-   _____
ment, supplies, activities, etc.

Purchase, store, and distribute equipment, materials, and supplies   _____

Arrange for food service   _____

Arrange for other services:
   Laundry   _____

   Diaper   _____

   Garbage   _____

   Utilities   _____

Custodial work, indoor and outdoors   _____

b. How often does the staff meet together?   _____

c. Do the teachers plan ahead for program activities?   _____

d. Number the following items as to their order of importance from the viewpoint of the administrator.

_____ 1. A well-qualified staff

_____ 2. An adequate facility (building, furnishings, and outdoor area)

_____ 3. Budget

_____ 4. Type of children in the program

_____ 5. Amount of money taken into the program (fees, donations, grants, etc.)

_____ 6. The program plan for the children

EVALUATION:

1. Describe the job of an administrator for a children's center.

2. List five major qualifications for an administrator.
   a.

   b.

   c.

   d.

   e.

(Administration: Operating a Children's Center—continued)

3. Outline the operation of a children's center.

Name _____ Date _____

Course _____ Experience # _____

PROGRAM MANAGEMENT

(To accompany Chapter 19)

OBJECTIVES:

- Identify and discuss the basic principles of managing a children's program.
- Describe components of management including team planning and teaching, room arrangements, and use of equipment and materials.

SETTING:

Type of situation (care center, family day care home, nursery, preschool, kindergarten, Head Start,

other) _____

Other information _____

Number of children present _____ Number of adults _____

Names and ages of children observed:

1. _____ Age _____

2. _____ Age _____

3. _____ Age _____

Time of day _____

TASK:

As you participate in or observe the program, respond to the following items:

Program Planning

1. Describe the kind of program planning that takes place. Who is responsible for the *planning*? Monthly:

Weekly:

Daily:

(Continued on next page)

Team Planning and Teaching

2. Describe the plan for working with children.
   Who is in charge?

   What does each adult do?

   Do the adults work independently? _____ Do the adults work as a team? _____

Room Arrangement

3. Draw a sketch of the room arrangement for the program. Label the interest areas.

Name _____ Date _____

(Program Management—continued)

Equipment and Materials

4. On Chart 19-A make a list of the visible furnishings, equipment, and materials in the area used for art activities.

Chart 19-A
ART ACTIVITY AREA

Furnishings	Equipment	Materials

EVALUATION:

1. Describe what is meant by management of a children's program.

(Continued on next page)

2. Briefly discuss three components of a program that are included in the management of children's activities:

   a. Team planning and teaching:

   b. Room arrangement:

   c. Use of equipment and materials:

Name _____ Date _____

Course _____ Experience # _____

PROGRAM MANAGEMENT: CHILDREN'S ACTIVITIES
(To accompany Chapter 19)

OBJECTIVES:
- Identify program goals and explain how they are achieved in the program.
- Describe components of the program including individual and group activities, routines and schedules, and evaluation.

SETTING:
Type of situation (care center, family day care home, nursery, preschool, kindergarten, Head Start, other)_____

Other information _____

Number of children present _____ Number of adults _____

Names and ages of children observed:

1. _____ Age _____

2. _____ Age _____

3. _____ Age _____

Time of day _____

TASK:
As you participate in the program, respond to the following items:

Goals

1. On Chart 19-B briefly identify what you think the goals of this program are. Give examples of the children's activities that lead toward these goals.

Chart 19-B
PROGRAM GOALS

List of Goals	Examples of Activities Leading to Goals

Individual and Group Activities

2. What type of groupings of children did you observe?

What kind of activities occurred with individual children?

What kind of activities occurred with small groups?

What kind of activities occurred with large groups?

Name _____ Date _____

Children's Activities

3. Observe children's activities in the interest areas listed on Chart 19-C. Give an example of how development is promoted in each area. Check the areas of development that you see promoted in each place. (Notice the example.)

Chart 19-C
DEVELOPMENT PROMOTED IN INTEREST AREAS

Interest Area	Area of Development							
Give an example of how development was promoted in each area.	Concept Formation	Problem Solving	Language Skills	Sensory Perception	Living Skills	Self-Concept	Motor Coordination	Expression of Feelings
Home Living *Example: Timothy played dress-up. With a doll, he imitated the role of his mother as she fed the baby. He talked as if he were the mother. He showed love and affection for the baby (doll).*	√		√	√	√			√
Art and Creative Media								
Listening and Reading								

(Continued on next page)

Chart 19-C
DEVELOPMENT PROMOTED IN INTEREST AREAS Continued

Interest Area	Area of Development							
Give an example of how development was promoted in each area.	Concept Formation	Problem Solving	Language Skills	Sensory Perception	Living Skills	Self-Concept	Motor Coordination	Expression of Feelings
Carpentry and Woodworking								
Manipulative and Table Activities								
Block and Large Toys								

(Continued on next page)

246

(Program Management: Children's Activities—continued)

Chart 19-C
DEVELOPMENT PROMOTED IN INTEREST AREAS Continued

Interest Area	Area of Development							
Give an example of how development was promoted in each area.	Concept Formation	Problem Solving	Language Skills	Sensory Perception	Living Skills	Self-Concept	Motor Coordination	Expression of Feelings
Science								

Adult-Child Interaction

4. Did individual children receive special attention or help? Give examples.

(Continued on next page)

Group Interaction

5. How did groups of children receive attention or help? Give examples.

Routine and Schedules

6. Did the children's activities have a schedule and/or a routine? Explain by giving an example.

Did the children seem secure and comfortable? _____ Explain by giving an example.

Child-Adult Ratio

7. What were the child-adult ratios in the children's program? List them on Chart 19-D.

Chart 19-D
RATIO OF CHILDREN TO ADULTS

Ages	Ratio	
Infants under 6 weeks	_____ children	_____ adults
6 weeks—18 months	_____ children	_____ adults
18 months—3 years	_____ children	_____ adults
3 years	_____ children	_____ adults
4 years	_____ children	_____ adults
5 years	_____ children	_____ adults
Combined ages	_____ children	_____ adults

(Program Management: Children's Activities—continued)

Assessment

8. What other ways can you suggest for achieving the same goals with the children in this program?

How did the staff evaluate the program?

Met in a group after the children went home. _____

Talked informally about the activities while the children were involved. _____

Talked informally about the activities after the children went home. _____

Wrote a summary of each child's progress at the end of the day. _____

Talked about certain children and how they could be helped. _____

Did not appear to evaluate the activities or the children's progress. _____

Explain other ways the program was assessed.

(Continued on next page)

EVALUATION:

1. Explain what a program goal is and write five goals for a day care center for children ages two to four years.

2. Develop an overview of a children's program. Include the components, children's activities, sample routine and schedule, and a way to assess the program.

Chapter 20
Evaluating Children's Programs

Evaluation is a procedure which helps determine the extent of a program's success. It examines the program's progress in achieving the goals which it claims to support. Evaluation requires the observer to look objectively at the total situation. This means making judgments based on the center's proclaimed program. Judgments are not based on the observer's personal convictions about what the program should be like.

The evaluation process is a system for seeing strengths and weaknesses of a center. The process identifies the strengths and weaknesses which relate to those goals the program says it is designed to accomplish. One safe assumption can be made. It is that the program exists first for the overall purpose of serving children and their families.

Of course, parents who are looking for a center can be more subjective. They are interested in a place for their children. The program must be in line with their family goals and expectations. Parents, therefore, evaluate a center on the basis of what they want for their own children. They want to know that the goals of the center are similar to their goals.

As you determine the success of a program, first identify your role. Are you evaluating as a parent looking at a place for your child? Or are you evaluating as a person studying child development and programs for children?

More than one visit may be needed to evaluate a program. This will depend on the length of your visit. It will also depend on the type of

Watch for clues about how adults provide guidance without detracting from each child's uniqueness.

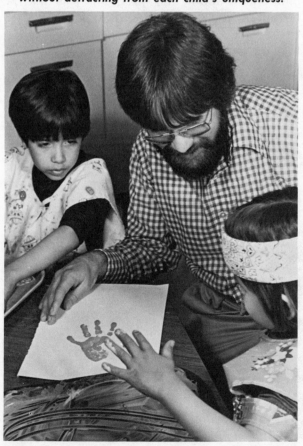

Are materials and equipment arranged for easy reach by children? Are they appropriate for the children's stages of development? Lisa appears to be comfortable in this setting, doesn't she?

253

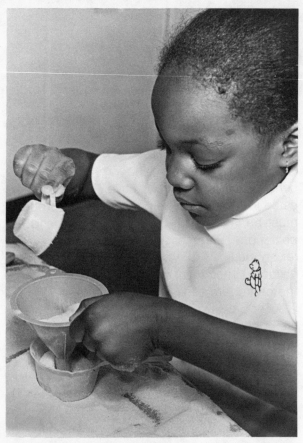

Do children have opportunities to learn by exploring on their own?

Is the program accomplishing the goals it proposes for the children? Are there opportunities for parents and others to talk with the staff about the program?

evaluation you are making. You will need to observe children and adults interacting with each other. You will also want to see how children play with each other. Of course, you will need to get a good picture of both indoor and outdoor facilities. Some centers provide printed information about their program. This will be helpful as you evaluate the program.

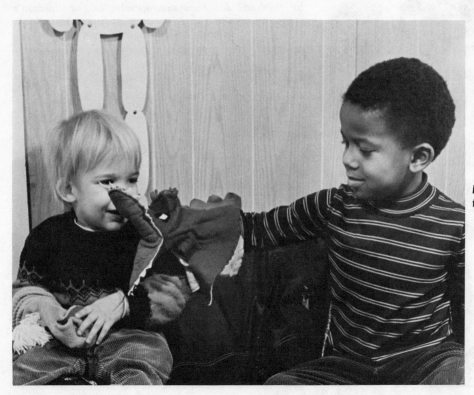

Do children have opportunities to learn through interaction with each other?

Name _____   Date _____

Course _____   Experience # _____

EVALUATING PROGRAMS

(To accompany Chapter 20)

OBJECTIVES:
- Identify and describe the components of a children's program.
- Describe the process of evaluating a children's program.

SETTING:

Type of situation (care center, family day care home, nursery, preschool, Head Start, kindergarten,

other)_____

Other information _____

Number of children present _____   Number of adults _____

Names and ages of children observed:

1. _____   Age _____

2. _____   Age _____

3. _____   Age _____

TASK:

Observe a children's program in your community and respond to the items below.

Program Goals

1. On Chart 20-A list the goals for the children in the program where you observe or participate. Give examples of how the program helped children work toward the goals. (Notice the examples.)

Chart 20-A
HOW PROGRAM HELPED CHILDREN

Program Goals	Activities
Example: Language skills	*Adults talked with children while playing with them.*

2. Did someone in the program explain the goals to you or did you identify them by observing? (*For example, if they said the goals included motor and cognitive skills, you look for examples of how children experience motor and cognitive activities. If the goals are not identified, you identify them by whatever the activities reveal.*) List the goals and give examples of children's activities that support the goals.

Evaluating a Program

3. List the things you considered when evaluating this program. (How did you know whether or not the program was succeeding in what it claimed it was doing?)

(Evaluating Programs—continued)

4. Evaluate one component of a children's program by listing your observations on Chart 20-B. (Notice the example.)

Chart 20-B
EVALUATING ONE PROGRAM COMPONENT

Component	Your Observation
Example: Food service	Food was served by adults.
	Children did not help set table or serve.
	Children ate in a room separate from their activity area.
	Children were not encouraged to talk about the foods they had.
	Adults poured milk for each child.
	Adults helped to serve foods on each child's plate.
	Adults helped spread butter on bread.
	Children did not help clear table at end of meal.
	The food service program was planned for serving children in the shortest time possible and with the least amount of confusion possible.
	The food service component was not planned to help children develop concepts or ideas about food.
	The children were not able to use the mealtime as a very meaningful learning experience.

(Continued on next page)

Chart 20-B

EVALUATING ONE PROGRAM COMPONENT Continued

Component	Your Observation

(Evaluating Programs—continued)

Interest Areas and Goals

5. On Chart 20-C list the interest areas for children's activities and briefly describe how each supported the program goals.

Chart 20-C
HOW AREAS SUPPORTED GOALS

Interest Area	Activities that Supported Goals

EVALUATION:

1. Briefly describe five components of a children's program.
   a.

   b.

(Continued on next page)

c.

d.

e.

2. Give three suggestions for evaluating a children's program.
   a.

   b.

   c.

Name _____   Date _____

Course _____   Experience # _____

EVALUATING THE OBSERVATION AND PARTICIPATION EXPERIENCES

Feedback is helpful for improving your observation skills and for increasing your effectiveness as you participate in children's activities. Fill out the form below. Do not sign your name.

1. What were the strengths of your observation and/or participation experiences as you studied children's development?

2. What were the weaknesses of your observation and/or participation experiences?

(Continued on next page)

3. What do you suggest to make the observations and participation more interesting and meaningful?

4. Rank the effectiveness of the experiences. Circle the mark that reflects your thinking.

Low   Moderate   High

```
    0       1       2       3       4       5       6
```

They did not change my level of understanding or my knowledge about children.

They increased my knowledge and understanding of children's development and behavior.

Selected Bibliography, Annotated

Almy, Millie, and Cunningham, Ruth. *Ways of Studying Children.* New York: Teachers College Press, 1969. A manual for studying about how children behave, feel, and think. Emphasis on skill in observation and study techniques.

Cahoon, Owen. *Cognitive Tasks. Teacher's Guide to Cognitive Tasks for Preschool.* Provo, Utah: Brigham Young University Press, 1974. Practical information on the cognitive development of young children with examples of everyday experiences and activities for children. Easy to read with attractive photographs of children in action.

Carbonara, Nancy. *Techniques for Observing Normal Child Behavior.* Pittsburgh: University of Pittsburgh Press, 1961. Principles and techniques for observing young children of varying ages and in settings such as nursery school, elementary classrooms, hospitals, and child groups.

Cohen, Dorothy H., and Stern, Virginia. *Observing and Recording the Behavior of Young Children.* New York: Teachers College Press, 1958. Details of observing and recording techniques. Information about children through observations of their movements and vocalizations. Helps reader to see children thinking and socializing with their bodies. View of struggles and success experienced by young children.

Dinkmeyer, Don C. *Child Development—The Emerging Self.* New York: Prentice-Hall, Inc., 1965. A basic text on child development. Includes observation techniques for the study of development and behavior.

Dinkmeyer, Don, and McKay, Gary D. *Raising a Responsible Child.* New York: Simon and Schuster, Inc., 1973. Practical steps to successful family relationships. Handbook for parents with methods that benefit parent and child.

Draper, Mary Wanda, and Draper, Henry E. *Caring for Children.* Peoria, Illinois: Chas. A. Bennett Co., Inc., 1975. A warm and realistic approach to the tasks of caring for children. Actual examples of child and adult interactions and experiences. Easy-to-read text with emphasis on development, behavior, activities for children. Managing and operating children's programs. Detailed appendix with practical information for parents and child care workers.

Fraiberg, Selma H. *The Magic Years.* New York: Charles Scribner's Sons, 1968. Practical illustration of first five years of life and the child's earliest conception of the world. Tells the story of personality development during the first five years. Describes and discusses typical problems that emerge with each stage of development.

Ginott, Haim. *Teacher and Child.* New York: Macmillan Publishing Co., Inc., 1972. Offers tools and skills for dealing with daily situations and psychological problems faced by all teachers. For parents and teachers, the simple-to-read book is written with grace and humor. Rich with anecdotes, stories, dialogue, and short scenarios.

Gordon, Thomas. *Parent Effectiveness Training.* New York: Peter H. Wyden, Inc., 1970. A common sense system for settling conflicts between parents and children. Emphasizes democratic discipline. Uses lively case histories. Presents a step-by-step method for negotiating solutions to conflicts.

Hildebrand, Verna. *Guiding Young Children.* New York: Macmillan Publishing Co., Inc., 1975. Focuses on interpersonal interaction of adults with infants and preschool children. Provides basic guidelines for giving children care and help for optimal growth in all areas of development.

Muller, Philippe. *The Tasks of Childhood.* New York: McGraw-Hill Book Co., 1969. Brings together various aspects of child development and examines them from a single viewpoint. Outlines theory, history, and vocabulary of child psychology. Ideas of Freud, Piaget, Lewin, and others are summarized and compared.

Osborn, Janie Dyson, and Osborn, D. Kieth. *Cognitive Tasks: An Approach for Early Childhood Education.* Athens, Georgia: Edu-

(Continued on next page)

cation Associates, 1974. Application of Piagetian theory to tasks of young children. Examples of everyday experiences and activities for children. Easy to read with practical information for teachers and students in early childhood development. (Available from publisher.)

Pulaski, Mary Ann. *Understanding Piaget.* New York: Harper and Row, Publishers, Inc., 1971. An introduction to children's cognitive development. Explanation of Piaget's theories of cognition in simple language. Emphasizes common stages of development and how children learn through play.

Redl, Fritz, and Wineman, David. *When We Deal with Children.* New York: The Free Press, 1972. Concrete illustrations of daily events of the professional and children. Reflects viewpoints of variety of disciplines. Observation techniques and what to look for when working with children.

Schwebel, Milton, and Raph, Jane. *Piaget in the Classroom.* New York: Basic Books, Inc., 1973. Application of Piaget's ideas in the contemporary school. Focuses on the transition from theory to practice. Concrete approach to the study of children's intelligence and knowledge.

Torrance, E. Paul. *Guiding Creative Talent.* Englewood Cliffs, New Jersey: Prentice-Hall, Inc., 1962. Shows how to identify and guide a wide range of creative talent at all age and educational levels. Proposes original approaches for handling needs and problems of the gifted.

White, Burton L. *The First Three Years of Life.* Englewood Cliffs, New Jersey: Prentice-Hall, Inc., 1975. Detailed guide to the intellectual, social, and emotional development of the very young child. Identifies developmental phases of the first three years with a thorough description of the characteristic physical, emotional, and mental developments. Instructions for parents concerning child-rearing practices, including selection and use of toys and equipment.

INDEX

Entries marked by an asterisk appear in explanatory matter, not in experience units.

A

Accident prevention, 71*
Acting out stories, 171. *See also* Dramatic play
Activities, 53, 55, 77, 78, 243–251, 255. *See also* Activity areas, Interest areas, *and specific types of activities*—Art, Blocks, *etc.*
Activity area, 85–89, 241. *See also* Interest areas
Administration, 229–231*, 233–237
Adult
  response to, on center staff, 235
  role of, at mealtime, 197
  role of, in child's self-concept, 98
  role of, in communication development, 179
  role of, in emotional development, 202*, 203, 204, 209
  role of, in infancy, 99*, 101*, 103, 106
  role of, in language development, 177, 178, 184, 186
  role of, in learning behavior, 212*, 217–219
  role of, in program planning, 240
  role of, in socialization, 189–193
Adult-child communications, 180
Adult-child interaction, 27, 247
Adult-child relations as influence on emotions, 206–209
Age concepts, 164
Aggression, 205
Alertness of infant, 105
Anecdotal record, 10*, 22
Animals, grouping, 171
Anxiety, 205
Appearance, in relation to development, 35*
Aquariums, 229*
Areas. *See* Activity areas *and* Interest areas
Art, 78, 88, 214, 216, 229*, 230*, 241, 245. *See also specific activities and supplies*—Painting, Clay, *etc.*
Assessment of program, 249, 251
Auditory concepts, 165. *See also* hearing
Auditory toys, 104
Autonomy, or selfhood, 91*

B

Beads, stringing, 86
Behavior, 5*, 211*, 212*, 213–221
  emotional, 205, 206
  influences on infant's, 103
  of a healthy child, 73
  social, 187–193
  unusual, 26
  while eating, 195–198
Block area, 61, 229*, 246
Blocks, 78, 86, 225
Body
  and senses, 107–109
  use of, during activity, 21
  use of, to solve problems, 133, 141
Body movements
  and self-image, 93*
  control of, 99*, 115*
  creative, 226
  infant's, 111, 113
Body parts, concepts of, 163, 170

C

Carpentry, 86, 87, 229*, 246. *See also* Woodworking
Case study, 3*
Cause and effect, awareness of, 170*
Checklists, 12*, 13*
Checklist
  for observing children, 28–30
  of thinking skills, 159–171
  on self-confidence, 97
Child-adult ratio, 248
Child care centers, 187*, 188*. *See also* Children's center *and* Program
Children's center, 219, 233–237. *See also* Child care center *and* Program
Classification, 58*, 138, 143, 144, 150, 162
Clay, 78, 88, 225, 226
Clothes, as help or hindrance to development, 21

Coins, identifying, 171
Collages, 78
Color, 58*, 138, 160, 188*
Communication
  child's need for effective, 179–182
  controlled verbal, 173*
  while eating, 196, 197
  See also Language
Components of children's program, 243, 251,
    255, 257, 259
Concentration, activities requiring, 78
Concept areas, 159–171
Concept formation, 137, 138, 143–151, 229*,
    230*, 245–247
Concepts
  and ideas, 62
  polar, 176
  relational, 143–147, 150
  use of, in language, 175, 178
  See also Self-concept
Conclusions, 9*, 23
Concrete experiences, as aid to development,
    59*, 60*
Confidence
  and support, needed by children, 39*
  in children, importance of having, 93*
  See also Self-confidence
Confidential information, 15*
Conflict, 216
Consistency, 212*, 213, 219
Controlled observations, 11–13*
Cooking, 78, 85, 87, 229*
Cooperation, 219
Cooperative play, 215
Coordinated movements of infant, 108, 109
Coordination, 57*, 99*, 195, 199
  eye-to-hand, 61, 64, 78, 115*, 116*
  motor, 125–131, 245–247
Coordinator, 234
Counting, 171
Creative activities, 214, 216
Creative media, 78, 88, 229*, 230*, 245
Creativity, 223*, 224*, 225–228
Cuddling behavior of infant, 106
Curiosity, shown by child, 21
Curriculum, 55. *See also* Activities
Cutting, 78, 88, 225, 226

D

Daily living skills, 189–193, 195–199

Daily schedule, 229*
Day care center, 250. *See also* Children's center
Dependence on others, 205
Description, 12*
Development, 5*, 13*, 39*
  areas of, 35*, 44
  clues to, 33*
  emotional, 35*, 201*, 202*, 203, 209
  hindered by changing goals, 48*, 49*
  insight to, gained through observing, 23
  intellectual, 133–135*, 137–142, 159, 172
    and concept formation, 143–151
    and levels of representation, 153–157
    and thinking skills, 159–172
  motor, 115*, 116*, 117–124
  motor coordination, 125–131
  observing, 27–31
  of communication skills, 182
  of infant, 99–101*
  of language, 174*, 175–178, 183–186
  promotion of, in interest areas, 245–247
  sequence of, 117–124, 133–135*, 141, 142,
    172
  through play, 43, 61*
Developmental tasks in speech and language,
    184, 185
Diary-type record, 10*
Director of children's center, 233, 235
Discipline, patterns of, 219
Dolls, playing with, 85
Dramatic play, 61, 62, 85, 86, 215, 225, 229*.
    See also Acting out stories
Drawing human figures, 168
Dressing, 189, 191, 192, 219. *See also* Dra-
    matic play

E

Eating, 189, 195–198
Egocentricity, 133
Emotional development, 35*, 201*, 202*, 203,
    209
Emotions, 203–209. *See also* Feelings
Environment, 229*
  and learning, 143, 150
  safe, 81–85
Equipment, 229*, 231*, 239, 241, 242
Evaluation, 5*, 243, 253*, 254*
Evaluating
  observation and participation experiences,
    261, 262

participation, 44–46
programs, 249, 253*, 254*, 255–261
yourself as an observer, 22
Exceptional behavior, 211*
Experience, influence on intellectual development, 133
Experiences, 3*, 4*
concrete, as aid to development, 59*, 60*
evaluating, 261, 262
Eye movement, 109, 170
Eye-to-hand coordination, 61, 78, 115*

F

Facial expressions, 161
Facilitator, participant as a, 39*
Family, 187*, 188*
goals and expectations of, 253*
importance of, to infant's development, 99–101*
Fantasy, 205, 224*
Fear, 205
Feelings, 201*, 202*, 203, 204, 211*, 212*, 213–216, 225, 228
expression of, 21, 40*, 245–247
of observer, role of, 23
See also Emotions
Fine motor activities, 115*
Fine motor control, 125, 127–130
Finger painting, 225
Finger plays, 64
Fish, feeding, 87
Focus of program, 53
Food
experiences, 225
service of, 257
Foods, categorizing, 169
Freedom, 226
needed by child, 40*
of expression, 212*, 228
Frustration, 205
Furniture, children's, safety features of, 90

G

Games, 229*
Goals
changing, as hindrance to development, 48*, 49*

for children, 47–49*
program, 47*, 51–55, 229*, 243, 249, 250, 253*, 254*, 255, 256, 259
Grasping, 108
Gross motor activities, 115*
Gross motor control, 125, 127–130
Group
activities, 243, 244
interaction, 248
Grouping. See Classification
Growth, 5*

H

Hammering, 78, 86
Happiness, 201*, 205
Hazardous surroundings, 71*
Hazards, safety, 85
Health
and activities, 77, 80
and safety, 71*, 72*
habits, 77, 79
Healthy child
behavior of a, 73, 75
signs of a, 74, 75
Hearing
and grasping, 108
of infant, 104
used in play, 57*
See also Auditory concepts
Home-living area, 61, 245
Homemaking, 229*
Home setting, 219
Human figures, drawing, 168
Hurlock, Elizabeth, 174*

I

Ideas, 223*, 224*, 225–227
and concepts, 62
forming, 137
Imitation, 150
Index level of representation, 135*, 154, 156
Individual activities, 243, 244
Infancy, 99–101*, 103, 106
Infant
body movements of, 113
comforting of, 103, 104
coordinated movements of, 108, 109

Infant [cont'd]
  coordination skills of, 57*
  eye movement of, 109*
  importance of adult to, 106
  memory development in, 100*
  motor skills of, 117–119
  mouth exploration of, 57*
  need of, for adult care, 103
  protection of, from hazards, 71*, 72*
  reflex action of, 107
  response of
    in awakened state, 105
    to adults, 104, 105
    to objects, 107
    to toys, 104, 111, 112
    while sleeping, 105
  sensorimotor characteristics of, 107–109
  sensory activities of, 57*
  use of body with play objects, 111, 112
  use of senses by, 113
Inferences, 10*
Inferiority, reasons for feelings of, 92*
Information
  obtaining, 21
  recording observation, 15*, 16*, 23, 25
Intellectual development, 133–135*, 137–142
  and concept formation, 143–151
  and levels of representation, 153–157
  and thinking skills, 159–172
  capacities in relation to, 35*
  factors influencing, 133
Interaction
  adult-child, 247
  group, 248
Interest, shown by child, 21
Interest areas, 52*, 139, 148, 149, 229*, 230*,
    240, 245–247, 259. See also Activity areas
Interest span, 226
Inventory of motor skills, 115*, 117–123

J

Joy, 201*, 202*, 205

K

Kindergartner, motor skills of, 121–123
Knowledge, social, 188*

L

Labeling, of objects, 188*
Labels, 178
Lacing activities, 86
Language, 173*, 174*
  as social tool, 188*
  beginning of, 101*
  simple, needed in participation, 39*, 40*
  skills, 61, 65, 93*, 175–178, 183–186, 229*,
    245–247
Learning, 5*, 39*, 57–60*, 61–69
Length of observation, 17*
Levels of learning, 133–135*, 141, 142
Levels of reality, 153–157
Levels of representation, 153–157
Library/reading center, 229*
Life-style, 91*
Limits, setting, 212*
Listening activities, 78, 89
Listening and reading area, 245
Listening skills, 64
Living skills, 245–247
Location, sentences indicating, 176
Logical thinking, 58*

M

Management, 229–231*, 239–251
Manipulative activities, 86, 229*, 246
Manipulatives, 78
Matching concept, 171
Materials. See Equipment
Maturation, 5*, 133
Mealtime, 195–198
Measuring, 78, 87
Memory, of infant, 100*
Mind, 100*, 133
Modeling, 112, 144, 150, 177, 178
Models, 211*
  adults as, 202*
  learning from, 71*, 72*
Money, concept of value of, 171
Motion concepts, 166, 167
Motivation
  and communication skills, 182
  role of, in language development, 183, 184
Motor activities of infant, 113, 114

Motor skills, 78, 111, 115*, 116*, 117–131, 195, 196, 199, 245–247. *See also* Muscle control *and* Movement
Movement of infant, 99–101*, 108, 109. *See also* Motor skills
Muscle control, 61. *See also* Motor skills
Music and creative movements area, 229*
Music time, 64

N

Naptime, 219
Negative behavior, 211*, 213, 217, 220, 221
Negative emotions, 203–207, 209
Negative feelings, 201*, 202*
Negativism, 91*
Number concepts, 138, 167, 169
Nutrition, as example of goal, 48*, 49*

O

Objective, importance of being, 18*
Objectives, 5*
Object level of representation, 135*, 153, 155
Object permanence, 100*, 112
Objects
    as aids to development, 59*, 60*
    as understood by child, 133
    classifying, 162
    concepts about, reflected in words, 175
    labeling of, 178, 188*
    representation of, 153–157
    response of infant to, 107
Observation
    basic to study of children, 9*
    definition of, 3*, 5*
    developing skills in, 25
    experiences, evaluating, 261, 262
    information, 15*, 16*, 19, 20, 23, 25–27
    length and range of, 17*, 18*, 31
    observer's behavior during, 15*, 16*
    of development, 27–31, 184, 185
    of levels of representation, 155, 156
    of one child, 25, 26
    qualities of an accurate, 31
    techniques, 10–13*
Oneness, concept of, 170
One-parent families, 188*

Operation of a children's center, 233–237
Outdoor play, 77
Outdoor play areas, safety features of, 90

P

Painting, 78, 225, 226
Paints, 88
Pairs, recognizing, 169
Parent, 124
    as influence on infant's behavior, 103
    as social influence, 187*, 188*
    evaluation of center by, 253*, 254*
    help of, in communication, 179, 182
    responsibility of, to infant, 99–101*
Parent-child activities in speech and language, 184, 185
Parenting, 3*
Participant
    responsibility as a, 39*
    role of the, 33*, 40*
Participation
    applying knowledge through, 9*
    definition of, 3*, 5*
    evaluating, 40*, 44–46, 261, 262
    experiences, recording, 33*
    guidelines for behavior during, 33*
    preparation for, 36*, 37*, 39*, 40*, 43
    questions to answer during, 35*, 36*
Pasting, 78, 88, 225, 226
Pegs and boards, 86
Pets, 87, 229*
Physical
    appearances, 74
    characteristics of a healthy child, 73
    skills, 78
Piaget, Jean, 133*
Place, prepositions to denote, 170
Plan, for activities, 53, 229*, 231*
Planning the program, 47–49*, 53, 239, 240, 242
Planting, 78, 87
Plants, 87, 229*
Play, 9*, 215, 219, 225, 228
    and development, 43, 57*, 58*, 68
    communication during, 179, 182
    development of language during, 178
    development of relational concepts through, 151

Play [cont'd]
  dramatic, 61, 62, 85, 86
  infant's, 100*, 101*
  infant's body movements during, 113
  infant's use of senses during, 113
  learning about safety through, 90
  learning through, 57–60*, 61–69, 138
  manipulative, 86
  outdoor, 77
  role of, in creativity, 223*, 224*
  role of, in emotional development, 203, 204, 209
  use of real objects in, 59*, 60*
  value of, 61
Playdough, 78, 88, 225, 226
Polar concepts, 176
Position, prepositions to denote, 170
Position concepts, 164, 165, 168
Positive behavior, 211*, 212*, 213, 217, 220, 221
Positive emotions, 203–206, 209
Positive feelings, 201*, 202*
Pouring liquids, 78
Practicum, 3*
Preparation for participation, 36*, 37*, 39*, 40*, 43
Prepositional statements, 176
Prepositions, use of, to denote place or position, 170
Problem solving, 63, 78, 137, 139, 140, 228, 245–247
Professional, responsibility to be, in participating, 33*
Program
  administration and management, 229–232*, 239–251
  components of, 255, 257, 259
  evaluation of, 253*, 254*, 255–261
  focus of, 53
  goals, 47–49*, 51–55, 229*, 243, 249, 250, 253*, 254*, 255, 256, 259
  plan, 53
  See also Children's center, operating a
Pushing-pulling, 111, 112
Puzzles, 78, 171, 229*

R

Ratio, child-adult, 248
Reading, 78

Reading area, 245
Reality, representation of, 153–157
Record and tape players, 64
Recording
  experiences, 33*
  observation information, 15*, 16*, 19, 20, 23, 25–27
  participation information, 33*
Reflex action of infant, 107, 109
Relational concepts, 143, 144–147, 150
Relationships and development, 35*
Representation, levels of, 153–157
Respect, 189, 212*
Responsibility as a participant, 39*
Romper, motor skills of a, 120, 121
Room arrangement, 52, 239, 240, 242
Routine, 229*, 243, 248, 251

S

Safety, 89, 90
  and health, 71*, 72*
  checklist, 81–84
  hazards, 85
  learning about, through play, 85–89
Sand play, 88, 225, 226
Sawing, 78, 86
Scales and checklists, 12*, 13*
Schedule, 229*, 243, 248, 251
Science
  activities, 87, 88
  area, 247
  center, 229*
Seasons, in relation to events, 168
Seeing and grasping, 108
Self, uniqueness of, 91*
Self-concept, 91–94*, 95–98, 125, 131, 201*, 229*, 245–247
Self-confidence, checklist on, 97
Self-discipline, 211*
Self-image, 92*, 93*, 95, 96, 98, 138
Senses, 61, 135*, 195, 199
  development of, 99–101*
  learning through the, 66, 67
  of infant, 99*, 100*, 107–109, 111–114
  used in play, 57*, 58*
Sensorimotor activity, 113
Sensorimotor characteristics, of infant, 107–109

Sensory
actions, 111
activities, 57*, 113, 114
acuity, 229*
experiences, 196
perception, 245–247
Sentences, 185. *See also* Language
Sequence of development, 133–135*, 141, 142
of motor skills, 117–124
of thinking skills, 172
Sequence of events, 171
Seriation, 58*, 138, 143, 145, 150
Sets, recognizing, 167, 170
Setting, 5*, 17*, 229*, 230*
describing the, 19
safe, 81–85, 89
Sewing, 86
Shape, 188*
concepts, 160
forming ideas about, 137
separating objects by, 58*
Sharing, 189, 215
Sign level of representation, 135*, 155, 156
Signs, 188*
of a healthy child, 74, 75
representing spoken word, 171
Size
concepts, 160, 161, 171
forming ideas about, 138
noticing differences in, 58*
Sleeping
patterns, 103, 106
response of infant while, 105
Snack time, 195–198
Social
knowledge, 174*, 188*
skills, 58*, 61, 65, 187*, 188*, 229*
transmission, influence on intellectual development, 133
Social-emotional development, 201*
Socialization, 187*, 188*, 195–199
Sounds, repetitious, infant's response to, 113
Spatial
concepts, 138, 143, 146, 151
relationships, 58*
Speech, 173*, 174*, 184, 185. *See also* Language *and* Language skills
Speed, concept of, 169, 170
Staff, 235, 249

Step-by-step process. *See* Sequence of development
Store/shopping center interest area, 229*
Storing equipment, 87
Story
acting out a, 171
time, 64, 214, 216
Stress, 180
Supplies. *See* Equipment
Symbol level of representation, 135*, 154, 156
Symbols, 173*, 188*

T

Table
activities, 246
area, 229*
Talents, use of, in participation, 36*
Tape recorder, 89, 229*
Tape recording, 4*
Tasks, 5*
Taste concepts, 163
Teacher, 234–236
Teacher-children activities in speech and language, 184, 185
Teaching, 239, 240, 242
Team
approach, 231*
planning, 239, 240, 242
teaching, 239, 240, 242
Temperature concepts, 165, 166
Temporal concepts, 143, 147, 151
Terrariums, 229*
Texture concepts, 165
Themes, special interest, 53*
Thinking, 137
Thinking skills, 61
checklist of, 159–171
development of, 57–60*
sequence of development in, 172
Time concepts, 59*, 138, 163
Time samples, 11*
Thoughts, expression of, by child, 40*
Toddler
motor skills of, 119, 120
possible hazards for, 71*
Toileting, 189–191
Toy area, 229*

Toys, 86, 215
    auditory, 104
    creative use of, 223*
    large, 246
    safety features of, 89
    sharing of, 189
    visual, 104
Tracking, 107–109
Trial and error, 141
Twoness, concept of, 170

V

Vice, using a, 87
Video tape recording, 4*

Vision
    infant's, 104, 105, 109
    used in play, 57*
Visual toys, 104
Vocabulary, 185. *See also* Language

W

Water and sand play area, 229*
Water play, 88, 225, 226
Weighing and measuring, 87
Weight concepts, 138, 167
Withdrawal, 205
Woodworking, 225, 226. *See also* Carpentry